Today's Shaman

Lana J Thomas

Published by Lana J Thomas, 2022.

While every precaution has been taken in the preparation of this book, the publisher assumes no responsibility for errors or omissions, or for damages resulting from the use of the information contained herein.

TODAY'S SHAMAN

First edition. March 21, 2022.

ISBN: 979-8201450359

Written by Lana J Thomas.

Table of Contents

Prologue

Consider how different the world is now when compared to how things were just ten years ago and then think back to twenty years ago. It is hard to comprehend the changes in values, lifestyles, and society. Consider how much family life has changed given the influx of technology, communication, and the internet. It is hard to believe that in the last twenty years alone, we have become accustomed to and reliant upon Google, YouTube, Twitter, Facebook, Kindle, Smart phones, and Smart TV.

We are deluged with information overload and as a result, regrettably, we are often too consumed by watching it or toying with gadgets to find the time necessary to expand our potential psychically, supernaturally, emotionally, and spiritually. The distraction of devices becomes retractive and intrusive. It can be disabling regarding evolving into who we can become because we waste so much time learning about who others is becoming and too little time discovering the self.

Consider how much our knowledge of the universes, planets, the cosmos, and our more immediate environment has changed. And still, the universe is full of secrets. There are so many truths humans are unaware of. However, because of technological advances, we are discovering new things with every passing moment. For example, we have had to relinquish much of what we believed about the solar system with the discovery of many new planets, the proof that dark matter exists and the discovery of super massive black hole 12 billion times as massive as our sun. As of April 2019- scientists have for the first time actually photographed a black hole, proving Einstein was right all along.

The information is exciting and confounding at the same time, because the more we discover, the more we learn how little we truly know. Change is a constantly confounding and as its pace becomes quickened, the direction it may be taking us could be beyond our comprehension. The confusion we experience may cause us to wonder what lies ahead and furthermore, why the knowledge is significant to us from a spiritual perspective. Do the changes and the new concepts we are discovering hold some dynamic truths that are important to our future as healers? I believe so!

When one considers the breadth of the universe and all its mysteries, the mind comes alive with the infinite possibilities. When one explores the possibilities of personal truths that may lie secreted within the All that Is...the truths reveal themselves and then seductively summon one even deeper into the abyss of the wondrous unknown where spiritual power awaits. Maybe you have felt the call to explore. Maybe you are uncomfortable with the changes as some do not seem positive and many results are confusing. Shifts in energy that cause disturbances in your life, your sleep, your work, and so, your desire for clarity has become more important than ever.

Intuitive people sense the transformations. Some may even literally feel the energy change creates. You could be one such person. Are there days when you feel anxious for no apparent reason? Do you notice you seem confused but do not understand why? Do you lack focus on those days and seem to be either very slow moving or lightheaded? This state can often be attributed to energetic wave patterns that are bringing about change. As the shift becomes a constant, that new wave pattern will ultimately settle in to become a new truth, a new result and—-an opportunity for even greater understanding of the universe we inhabit. Change takes many forms, and it is often hard to determine what is happening. Sometimes, just the awareness of something going on and an acceptance of the outcome (trust) is all that is required to be included in the flow, which is where one wants to be, of course.

The changes can be troublesome when people do not understand that energetic shifts cause temporary disruptions in thought patterns. Fortunately, understanding that change is constant grants intuitive spirits a connection to the fluctuations because our spiritual energy shifts and adapts to changes more readily just it was designed to do. It is important to note that the more aware one is of the energetic shifts 7 that are transforming our world the less they will have a negative effect on the body and mind. The more quickly we are willing to evolve, the less discomfort will be felt.

Introduction

During the journey to the pinnacle of our spiritual lives, we, like the mountain climber, must surmount barriers, attempt alternate routes, and persevere despite all odds. We navigate turn upon turn in attempts to find our path; the path we selected or the path that has been chosen for us. It is not always easy to determine one's purpose, but because you are reading this book about shamans, I believe it is a fair conclusion that you are drawn to the role of a healer, in some respect.

I wish to thank you for purchasing this eBook. I pray you find great value in its inspirational message for our future. I am certain that you know we are changing at an amazing pace and the more we implement all we are learning, the more we will escalate further necessary growth and expansion of our healing paradigm. This book is about the past and how it is being pulled forward into the mainstream of energy medicine, however you apply that in your life and practice. This book will show you the evolution of shamanic practices utilized for centuries and where it fits in our methods today. Are you one who is exuberant about change and mind expansion. Are you determined to develop your passion into a professional career?

If this is the case, I ask you now, "Have you determined that your gifts are sufficient for the path you feel led to? Do you think you are prepared or want to be prepared to embark on a journey of self-exploration to determine what gifts you possess or need to acquire to become the type of healer you are capable of being?" Do you possess the gifts necessary to see your way to the fruition of your goals? If you do not, would you like to?

The truth be told, if you are like most people, you are not quite sure how to answer those questions, although you are aware that you need to grow and expand your knowledge base. We all do! You see, 3 we are always in a state of growth and change. Change is the one constant in our lives. It is not something we can control, and change is, as it was designed to be, ever changing, constantly in flux, and presently, it seems to have accelerated to a pace that leaves our heads spinning.

My lifelong experiences with guided healing techniques have been the impetus for examining all opportunities and possibilities to expanding my skills and me dream of being a renowned energy healer. So, with that plan in mind, the archangels generously offered to assist me in writing this manuscript. The stressed the importance of its message. That said, let us move on into the future of energy medicine.

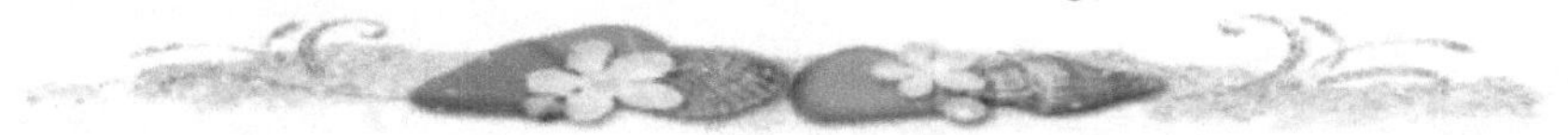

Part I: Change is Vital to the Evolution of Energy Medicine

Everything, as we know it, changes. Our environment, our bodies, our planet, our minds, the material and immaterial world, and what have you, are in a constant state of growth or decline, expansion or contraction, inclusion or exclusion, and addition or deletion. The one thing the universe is not, is stagnant. So, with the changes we may not see or understand, our own stagnation or being stuck, can be reflected in our angst or discomfort while we are caught helplessly in midst of the change that is happening all around us. If you know you are not evolving fast enough and still feel the shifts to a degree that leaves you befuddled, then like eagle on the winds of heaven, spread your wings and welcome change with and open mind and heart. Do you ever feel stuck or like you are missing something?

If you feel stuck, some force of change may be propelling you toward a growth spurt, a new idea, a higher truth, and a new you of some sort. The awareness that you feel stuck is an indication you do desire growth and higher self-awareness and you like going with the flow of energy. I know you do not want to be left behind so, if you are willing to explore where change may lead you then you will surely be offered the opportunity to accept the new change and benefit from its teaching. Why the emphasis upon change?

Well, to explain briefly, today's shamans know that we must cast off some of the old ways of conducting healing to accommodate the new attributes of healing powers that are being presented to us. If we cling to the old traditional and antiquated ways of healing then we may be caught in a place of decline and have missed the changes presented as growth and opportunities for expansion, inclusion, and addition. It is a new world, filled with new ideas, new concepts, new methods, and new and more powerful denser energy. If we are stuck solely in the old tried and true methods, we are also consequently stuck in the past.

"How Wonderful It Is That Nobody Need Wait a Single Moment Before Starting to Improve the World." -Anne Frank

Chapter One: Yesterday's Shaman

Did you know that based on historical accounts, Shamanism dates back 30,000 years to origins in Africa as evidenced by cave paintings that indicate a healer at work? Concrete evidence states that shamanism has existed for 10,000 years. According to Rosano (2006), "Evidence from Upper Paleolithic (UP) cave paintings suggest that these ideas may extend back tens of thousands of years". Regardless of the actual years of existence, there remains a vast amount of mysticism and romanticism connected to the ancient art of shamanism. We are enthralled with the power, the history of the paranormal, soul and out of body travel, and connection to the metaphysical that many shamans possess.

The definitions of shamanism are many, but all retain one common description; the shaman enters altered consciousness states to communicate with the spirit world to get information about how to heal. The obvious power they possess causes us to observe them in awe and wonder. The trust in its credibility and reliability is evident in its permanence. After thousands of years, it still exists and still is an effective form of healing. Its origins must have been built on a very solid foundation of trust in the unknown and the unseen. Shamanism is notably a form of mysticism. Mysticism is defined as: belief that union with or absorption into the deity or the absolute, or the spiritual apprehension of knowing inaccessible to the intellect, obtained through contemplation or surrender.

Shamanism is considered a form of folk religion or a religion which occurs in a small community which does not adhere to larger systems of religion. Shamanism has survived as the oldest/ancient religion.

Studying the most powerful shamans often instills in us a desire to possess those same marvelous spiritual abilities. We want to be like them, know what they know and experience what they experience. The personal experience may be the most enticing thing about the lives of shamans because they seem to be different than the average spiritualist. Shamans practice in realms reserved for the most highly attuned spiritual healers because they must work courageously with great faith and trust, given the fact that many transcend into frightening (sometimes) realms of unseen reality and time and space. Historically, some have depended upon ancient, even cave man fetishes to usher them to a dimension of the spirit world. For example, burning of sage and other herbs, shaking rattles and beating drums often escorts the shaman into an altered state of consciousness or supernatural awareness of higher intuition and wisdom. Shamans customarily carry a staff of some sort, and many adorn themselves in flowing robes with feathers and bones. They possess psychic abilities such as clairaudience, clairvoyance, remote healing, astral projection, and telepathy, to name but a few. Many have reported using psychedelic drugs such as mushrooms and/or peyote to connect to the spirit realm and to receive heightened awareness. However, with all the wonder of the life they live, they are unfortunately not fully accepted into modern society and are often discounted as too weird to be believable and possibly insane. (By closed minded people)

When you stand them beside a doctor in a white coat with a credible Ph.D. on his office wall, it is easy to understand how spiritual healers are often discounted as foolish or archaic. Nonetheless, many possess inexplicable healing power that is well researched, documented, proven and yet little understood—And, because there is scientific proof of the effectiveness of energetic healing it is becoming more acceptable and more available and acceptable. That shift is now apparent as an important change in the future of energetic healing.

Therefore, to gain even more credibility, some Shamans are choosing more accepted methods to integrate their practice more easily into society and thereby be of more service as healers. It is not a compromise; it is an accommodation to the needs of the sick and the fast-expanding role as an energetic healer. The apparel of leather and feathers and shaking rattles is obviously not well tolerated by the majority of people in our technologically advanced world. It is accepted in small circles and thus limited in its scope of practice. We can change that by adapting to the advanced energetic healing methods being offered by healer Guides and Angels.

Color and Sound Therapy is widely accepted.

Bringing shamanism to the forefront of energy healing today entails developing methods that promote our credibility as healers. We do not have to wear smocks with a stethoscope around our necks, but we need to look and act like professional healers if we want to be taken seriously by greater numbers of people who might benefit from understanding spiritual healing. Not only do we need to exhibit professionalism, but we also need to exhibit greater power and healing results. This is accomplished by letting the energy do the work and letting ascended healers support us more now than we have been able to because we were limited in our reach and ability to connect with them. As you read on, you will discover the validity of the tools for your work that are offered and impeccably supported by your etheric healing team.

Modern Shaman

The old ways of shamanic healing have served us well and they will continue to do so. They need never be discounted as ineffective and will even become enhanced. Some still deserve to be employed, however, if a shaman is determined to cling solely to ancient methods and ideas, he or she will miss the opportunity to learn new and more effective ways to work as today's shaman in today's technologically advanced society and world. Using solely traditional methods alone is like walking backward in hopes of moving forward. Furthermore, when we persist in restricting our acceptance to the old ways it is more difficult to learn from our spiritual guides and teachers who are living in a highly evolved everchanging environment of very high vibrational fields. Simply put, we must move forward now because we are on the cusp of an energetic healing revolution! "It is no secret that Energy Medicine is the future, even in conventional forms of medicine." <u>The American Board of Holistic Medicine</u>

So, the crux of the issue is, how far forward we move the healing power of shamanism is limited only to the scope of how open minded we can be about accepting instruction from modern day spiritual teachers. The teachers or guides have not changed, however, what they offer now has seemingly limitless boundaries for healers who are flexible and want to realize then employ the advanced denser forms of energy vibrations. And the more we are willing to learn, the more they will offer to teach. Your personal path (and your willingness to work at it) will dictate which direction the instruction and this book takes you on your journey of growth and expansion. Keep in mind...*it is all in your mind* and your mind is the doorway to knowledge and wisdom. Creation begins in the mind and expansion of the creation is furthered through thought, contemplation, study, and finally to practice. The mind is now clarified as that which we normally refer to as the soul. The eternal soul in fact, because it is our very essence, our being, and most evident in our present, our personality.

The mind is the aura, the energy field that is ours and ours as it exists as a part of the entire consciousness of the universe we inhabit. It is not our brain that controls our body and maintains its functionality. The mind is expansive and contractive. It can reach beyond the limits of a limited present to see within eternity and all that is. So, as you can clearly see, the mind is where we live, work, exist, flourish, or perish based upon the expanse of our minds. The voyage is exciting and thrilling. The experience can be a bit unsettling as you know. But it is a trip that really has no destination or end!

Don't you find that exciting?

Holding Truth as Our Own

Shamans are known to live on the edge of society. What we do privately in ceremony such as rattling, drumming, movement, dance, and meditation is sacred and our source of power but is not necessarily meant to be displayed. Admittedly, Shamans can be led to do some pretty weird things in private and that is how it is meant to be, but to make that public can often lessen the reputation of the shaman in much of society at large. It can also compromise your sacred ceremony that is held with your healing team and guides who are actively healing you.

The Value of Shamanism

"Having said that, we cannot dismiss shamanism as having no relevance to modern society. Obviously, it does, but this very much depends how you approach it. In an age where most information is transmitted via print or electronics, the value of adopting shamanic techniques lies in recovering knowledge from within, and also in relating with other people. Ecstasy can be freed from the purely private domain and returned to the communal. Also, in trying to regain the spirit of our collective past, we can regain a sense of community with our ancestors, using techniques which carry us back to our forebears on the savannah plains of Africa. this can endow us with a sense of community that surpasses all cultural differences. In learning to see the world as shamans, we reconnect with ourselves, and can adapt much easier to the world around us." The Value of Modern Shamanism by Phil Hine Walking Between The Worlds (netdna-ssl.com)[1]

Chapter Summary/Key Takeaways

Change is a very good thing. Without change we remain the same and we stagnate and lose interest in living life to its fullest potential. Change revels in heightened energy flow and it also provides the impetus to continue to grow into your highest self who knows no point in which a spiritualist can state, "I have arrived!" The Universes propose the truth in the scope of limitless potentials and limitless knowledge. Brilliant in its light...it beckons you forth.

- Whether you are contemporary and use eastern methods of

1. https://holybooks-lichtenbergpress.netdna-ssl.com/wp-content/uploads/Techniques-of-Modern-Shamanism-vol-1-Walking-Between-The-Worlds.pdf

Reiki or similar modalities such as acupuncture...you are limiting yourself in healing potential by clinging solely to the tried and true of the past.

- Certainly, the tried and true has a reputation you need not establish and yet, what lies ahead that is being offered now as an expansion of the knowledge we have held so dear.
- Are you a catalyst? Can you assist in the growth and evolution of healing? How else can we ever compete with western medicine which does harm?
- A 10-year study about prescription drugs revealed-illness related to medical treatment results in the leading cause of death in the USA. Specifically, adverse reactions to prescription drugs result in more than 300,000 deaths per year. (Null et all, 2003)
- No deaths result from alternative medicine which is preventative and proactive versus reactive and prescriptive in treatment models of pharmacology and allopathy. Follow the money to prescription drugs and find the source of agony in those who are energetically weak and shutting down.
- Ever heard? "We have a pill for that" and "If that pill bothers you with bad side effects, we have a pill for that!"
- We need not be seen as competing with allopathic medicine. We are deliberately offering alternative methods for those who seek a safe and less invasive path to healing.

It is okay to begin your journey today!

It is okay!

The mistakes you have made along the way are lessons, not failures. You were meant to get back up and find a way that resonates with you. There is no expiration date to reinventing yourself! That is a promise!

Chapter Two: Getting Started

The best time to begin your journey is now! Just think about the possibilities and begin making plans to become the powerful healer you have dreamed of being. Then, take your first step to reaching out to the cosmos and let your guides fill your open mind to overflowing. This exciting message is essentially what this book is about. Healing today is about using your mind to expand your ability to comprehend instructions and follow those who will teach you truly dynamic ways in which to conduct your healing adventures. In doing so, you help yourself as well, because this is how healers work best. Being the healer is never just about you and it is never just about your client, it is always about the All and your action's effects upon it.

Each step you are willing to take toward change opens a new door to further growth and effectiveness of the healing arts and your awareness sharpens the awareness of many other healers by shifting the collective consciousness. Dramatic changes are coming in our world and with those changes, we may find closer similarity to healing on a literal higher dimension by bringing the wisdom of higher knowledge into our dimension. This will happen naturally when we can raise our consciousness up to the same level of those who truly understand the extent of its power. Today's shaman has the potential to move beyond all genres of healing that we have experienced to date. The more the universe changes and we open our minds and hearts to the shifts, the more effective we will become.

We can expect the healing energy we will learn to conduct and control to exceed any that have been present in our lifetimes. Such is the promise of healing angels who come with the gifts of the "New Energy", as they refer to it. Because we are obviously shifting our thought to a higher dimension or density than we were previously granted access to, we are finding that we have been given access now. People like Corey Goode and David Wilcock (Gaia.com) believe that the opportunities for advanced thought, perception, and truth, if you will, have been offered more than once in times long past. Beings of other worlds and dimensions, being benevolent by nature, have offered to assist us in our spiritual growth. But, like many new concepts, such as angelic healing or extraterrestrial contact have been erringly turned into a form of religion. Religiousness is not the goal of those who bring the information. Freedom from restrictive thought, judgement, limited ability to explore the cosmos and rigid doctrines are what they desire.

One, anyone, must be free to define purpose, desire, and spiritual growth in order to complete the tasks they came here to do. Going outside the norm, just like folk religion, and staying free of boundaries are what grants limitless imagination, invention, creation, and exploration. Such freedom of thought garners new ideas, fresh promises of moving forward and better opportunities to exceed the limits of commonly held theories and beliefs. Such freedom grants that brilliant minds may conceive new inventions that alter our world and others who will assist in altering our consciousness to an even higher state. Those who lean toward advances in technology may invent healing devices that will help mankind live a more productive life.

Healers can take many forms and healing is not just about shamanism or one on one. Healers often see the world as their patient in need of assistance. Not all shamans will be widely known for their healing power. Some will live in divine obscurity while they learn more from other dimensions that can then be integrated into the collective consciousness. Do you have an idea of where you fit in? Do want to have a private practice? Do you want to be the sage in a cave and dwell in the densities that solitude can create? If you are uncertain, you need to ask your guides to direct you in every step you take so you know what goals to set. That is after all their job, and they are so good at it. Also, knowing that you are directly connected to Source in your meditations and constant communication will inspire you and direct you to the steps that will lead your success.

Getting Started by Defining your Aspirations

I assume you carefully and thoughtfully read the entire introduction, if not, please go back and do so now. Otherwise, you may miss a great deal of valuable information that prepares you for the journey this book will imminently take you on. I know that people like to jump right in and get started with learning and discovery, but you have time to take in the teachings here with patience and contemplation. Slow down and concentrate, so you do not miss a thing contained in the pages of this book. If you have thoroughly read the introduction, then please proceed. We move with deliberation and our concentration focused on possibility when we are pursuing a higher goal. We move with light when we pull our minds out of the darkness of the drama of life. We move in stealth through the days of our lives when we know we must carefully guard our spirit from deterioration and neglect.

We also move in joy when we are on a path that we are certain will lead us to a higher vibration and power. The pages herein contain knowledge that will forever change your life. I know that this can generate excitement, but I wish you to take this slow, so the energy does not overwhelm, because I promise you, it can. In the mere reading of this book, you will find that your vibration has been raised considerably and you will need to adjust and incorporate the new you into your life. Therefore, I ask that you proceed in steps, so your energy field has the time necessary to adjust to the flow and the power the energy patterns possess. Otherwise, you may become confused and uncomfortable physically. Energy is never to be trifled with and not taking it seriously shows a lack of understanding or respect for the powers one can possess and utilize. On a lighter note: You may be feeling the elation of your spirit given the possibilities that lie ahead.

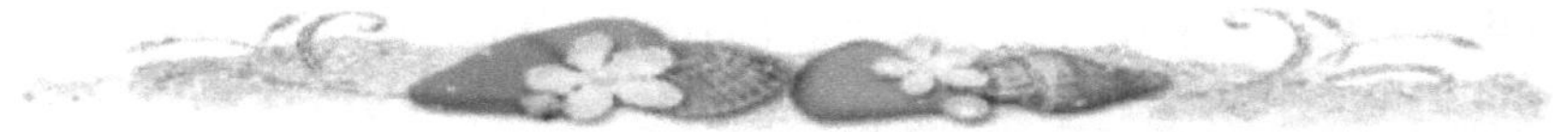

The First Step

Before you embark on your exploration of new ideas presented here, please take a few moments to write down your responses to the following topics:

- How you presently perceive healing?
- What techniques do you value most? and most importantly
- What do you do that sets you apart from other healers?
- In other words, "What techniques have you learned that are personal and privatized to you alone." This is your destiny and yours alone!

Now, write your theory of healing. Put it in a framework or a list and see how it looks. Is it all inclusive and adequate to meet the needs of all your clients or family? This may be something you have never considered in depth. This exercise is enlightening but can be difficult for some to formulate. It is worth doing for many reasons which will become evident.

Clarifying Your Destiny

Keep your list nearby, because you will want to keep what is evidentially yours and throw out what will no longer serve you well. The choices will naturally become clear to you. Maybe you will keep it all and expand your list and maybe you will delete many items you have tried but found wanting. All that Is in your personal space remains open to expansion or contraction, addition or deletion, inclusion or exclusion, but whatever you choose should forever bring about growth and never decline if you are on track and on your path to truth.

The Second Step:

Determine to discover your strengths and weaknesses so you can build upon your strengths. As you become stronger in your abilities and knowledge your weaknesses will subside and eventually fade away. Focusing on your weakest points is simply by the Law of Attraction holding them in your space. By pursuing your strengths, you will naturally attract strong guides and helpers who seek to build you up even more.

To elaborate on the point of strong helpers, have you clearly defined who your helper spirits are, and do you have a close personal relationship with each of them? It is becoming clearer that telepathic communication with your team is an important aspect of healing. Just as Shamans of old contacted the spirit realm for guidance, it is more important today to learn to communicate in conversation with your guides. It is the way of the future in the life a spiritual healer or initiate of any style. We are to learn to be more like advanced beings if we wish to thrive in the days and years ahead.

The Third Step:

Take a deep breath, relax, and telepathically ask your spiritual guides to help you along the way during your reading. Ask them to point out personal messages and then expand on them for your personal growth so you will move beyond what the words herein offer. This step is very important for the future of your new healing practice. Let them guide you on a personal level and in so doing, you will be strengthening the connection that will serve you while you are actively engaged in a future healing session or ceremony. This, dear reader, is the Key to your Success. Listen and pay attention to your guidance as this is the most effective tool you can possess as a Today's Shaman. You will want to write this down and leave a note on your desk that reminds you that-

Chapter Summary/Key Takeaways

- Become intimately acquainted with your guides so you know they have your best interest at heart and their purpose is to assist you in becoming your highest and best self.
- Remember to ask them to strengthen your gifts and be opened to receiving any instructions they are waiting to offer you. They will offer you whatever tools you need to be effective in your life and practice!

~Developing your ability to use your mind, telepathy, and etheric thought energy to exceptional levels are an imperative to Today's Shaman~

PART II: Universal Laws

Chapter Three: Understanding Mentalism

In the introduction, I alluded to the concept that healing is 'all in your mind.' It is not an easy concept to fully grasp because our minds are so complex, and the Collective Thought of the Universe is so vast an idea to consider that we can feel overwhelmed trying to comprehend it all. Mentalism, as Hermes called it, is a teaching dating back to Old Testament times in ancient Egypt. Historically, the powerfully creative Secrets of Hermeticism were revealed only to a select few initiates who would vow to protect them, and that practice remained for centuries.

The Hermetic Manual called The Kybalion, came eons later and was written by three men called only the 'Initiates'. It contains The Seven Sacred Principles taught by Hermes. Descriptions of Hermes and some background on his history "According to some myths, Hermes wasn't only a messenger of the gods, but also the inventor of speech. As such, he is often associated with oratory or interpretation. In Greece, an interpreter was called hermeneus, and today the science of interpretation is known as hermeneutics. Hermes was the only Olympian capable of crossing the boundary between the living and the dead and carrying the souls of the dead in Hades. In time, he came to be known as "the conductor" or "the leader of souls."

People also called him "patron of travelers and thieves," "shepherd of men," "trickster," and "Argus-slayer." (www.greekmythology.com) "He (Hermes) was also credited with inventing fire, dice (and so was worshipped by gamblers in his capacity as the god of luck and wealth), musical instruments, in particular, the lyre (made from a tortoise shell), and the alphabet. Famous for his diplomatic skills, he was also regarded as the patron of languages and rhetoric. Travelers regarded him as their patron, and stone pillars (hermae) with a phallus symbol were often to be seen set up along roadsides. In addition, Hermes was regarded as patron of the home and people often built small marble stelai (an upright rock or pillar) in front of their doors in his honor." (Ancient History Encyclopedia)

Figure 1 Hermes Trismegistus

The Seven Sacred Principles of Hermeneutics

The first of the Seven Sacred Principals is: The All is Mind -The Universe is Mental

The Universe is Mental

All that is, began with thought! Much like a painter creates his masterpiece in his mind before he puts his brush to the palette the All was created by thought and imagination or creative thought. The result will reflect what was conceived in the creator's mind. Creationism has been referred to, of late, as Intelligent Design; given that the perfect order of all things simply could not have been the result of chaos. The phrase was first coined by Charles Darwin in 1861 and was developed more fully in the late 1980's. It is a phrase used to dispute the existence of God by atheists and yet, it does convey the construct of thought having been involved in creation, even if the 'thinker' or God is annulled in the atheist's construct.

Such order emanated from an intelligence (thinker) at the very beginning of our existence and that extends to the vastness of the universes we have yet to understand, not to mention, explore. Mankind forever wrestles for a theory in which to prove our origins and understand our beginnings, but many now understand that though we cannot yet fully grasp how the All was created, we understand that the creator is within all of us because we all are the All (the Everything). We are each a nucleotide in the infinite DNA chain of life. Each one an individual in our own right, and yet intrinsically connected to everything and inseparable from it. Even in death!

Let me explain why I use that analogy. Many years ago, when I was at the beginning of my search for my calling and my true self, in a conversation with the Father (What I affectionately call Him), I asked him who he was. He stated, "Imagine if you will the vastness of the universes, planets, stars, constellations, and galaxies. Now imagine within that scene is a giant snake like creature undulating in space.

Look closer and see that the snake is really a massive DNA chain. And now, see that every tiny cell of that DNA chain is a person just like you. That DNA chain is comprised of all who exist and in that, that DNA chain is everything."

He graciously offered me an image similar to the one above that I could envision and begin to grasp as the infinite limitlessness of All that is and how it is all connected to form life. In the complexity of the design is a simple premise of Oneness with no breaks in the chain. To explain in another way, the universe is a swirling undulating mass of energy, etheric or thought energy that can be tapped into at any time. The All is all collective thoughts of all time, from the beginning of time and all knowledge exists for the taking from within it. Isn't that amazing! It is like Google on high vibration steroids. Knowledge is power because thought is the power used to create. Thus, the more we learn from the All, the more powerful we become. Understanding the Law of Mentalism is very complex, and it deserves your full attention, so I have included an excerpt from a book that sort of fell into my lap as I grappled with trying to understand what was being presented to me when I was asked to write this book. This century old book greatly helped me understand the concepts put forth by Hermes thousands of years ago. It is available free online in a Pdf format.

Excerpt from: The Law of Mentalism

A practical, scientific explanation of thought or mind force: the law which governs all mental and physical action and phenomena: the cause of life and death. *-VICTOR SEGNO*

"Mentalism is the harmonious action of the three most powerful faculties of the mental organization. The first of these is Thought, the second, Etheric Energy, and the third is will. Thought is the intelligence which is collected by the brain for the use of the mind, from such passing mental vibrations as are in harmony with it. Etheric Energy is the force generated in the brain by the process of thinking. It is upon this force that thoughts travel from the cells of the brain to their destination. The will is the operator and director and dispatches and guides the thoughts to their respective stations.

Thus, thought conveyed by Etheric Energy, and guided and controlled by Will, becomes a power of such magnitude that neither material nor distance are a barrier to its transmission. Thought produces energy and energy creates force, which in turn produces action and motion. Thought through motion displaces the atoms in the air which surrounds the body, thus causing vibrations or thought waves in the atmosphere. A weak thought makes only a slight displacement just as a faint breeze sway but gently the leaves of the trees; while strong, forceful thoughts displace the atoms over a greater area.

Marconi, the inventor of wireless Telegraphy, says that a word or its equivalent creates a vibration in the air just as a pebble thrown into a pond creates a ripple in the water, and that this vibration travels with the speed of lightning to the terminus, however distant and makes itself known and felt by every telegraph instrument that is tuned in harmony with the sender. In the same manner, a thought from the brain of one person travels on despite all resistance until it is taken up by the brain or brains that are in harmony with the mind from which it was sent.

A thought of scorn or praise, when sent by the will from the brain becomes a living force and is not lost in the multitude of sounds and vibrations but goes on to find the individual against whom or in favor of whom it was directed. Such thoughts strike the person with an impact which either hurts or helps them. Those who do not understand the Law of mentalism may not know when these thoughts have taken flight and for the same reason the person receiving them may not know from whence they came; nevertheless, he is either uplifted or depressed by them. Almost every person will admit to having often experienced a sudden depression of feeling, or a fear that something unfortunate had or was about to occur; and again, at another time of being controlled by a sensation of hope and happiness, even in the face of seemingly unpleasant facts, and with no apparent cause for it.

There are few people who have not been convinced at some time in their lives that they felt the thoughts of another influencing them, even when they knew that that person was a distance from them. Perhaps when deeply engrossed in work or study you have been startled by what seemed a living presence beside you, and the mental impression was so strong that you involuntarily reached out your hand as though to touch the living flesh, while your eyes were fixed upon space, and you saw more from within than from without.

Or perhaps you experienced this same feeling of nearness of some friend whom you believed to be far away, and in a few moments, he entered your presence and you in astonishment greeted him with "I was just thinking of you." These or similar experiences demonstrate to what extent a person is sensitive to Mentalism, and to what degree other people are able to influence his thoughts and actions for good or evil.

For the want of a better explanation, knowledge acquired in this way has been credited to Telepathy or Intuition, which means that it was gained through some faculty other than the five senses. It is a recognized truth that we cannot feel or know of that which does not exist; therefore, such experiences not only prove the existence of the power, but they prove that we have the faculty to perceive that power. As man possesses this faculty, it is his duty to develop and use it for his own advancement and for that of humanity. It is an indisputable fact that Thought is the foundation or creative force back of every action, whether it be the simple lifting of the hand, or that used to build a city.

The sculptor by his thoughts gives to his model shape and being ere he chisels it from the marble. The artist, likewise, had already created the picture in his brain by his thoughts before he attempted to reproduce it on canvas in colors. Statuary and pictures are but material reproductions of the artist's thoughts and should you ask him, he would tell you that they were but poor imitations of the mental pictures from which he copied them." In summation: I quote from The Law of Mentalism-Victor Segno

? Mentalism is power

? Mentalism is what you make of it

? Mentalism is limitless in its scope and imagination is the spark that ignites the fire from within your mind. Do not ever fear that what you are creating is just in your imagination! Imagination is key to finding the power to create healing energy!

? "Mentalism is the source of all intelligence and of physical, social, mental, spiritual, scientific, artistic and mechanical achievement and advancement. Just take a moment to consider that point. It will boggle your mind!

? Mentalism underlies all knowledge-

? Mentalism is the cause of all happiness or unhappiness, health or disease, success, or failure.

? Mentalism will be closely associated with our lives after we leave this earth.

? The power of mentalism is not for the few. If one can do it, all can do it if they have a strong will.

Examples include: ? Mesmerism ? Hypnotism ? Personal magnetism ? Magnetic healing ? Mental science ? Spiritualism ? Clairvoyance ? Clairaudience ? Telepathy ? Mediumship

Mentalism in its fruition is the power of the mind over the body. Just considering the power of those statements can rock one's world. Trying to grasp all the concepts put forth is mind blowing. One thing for certain, it is eye opening to realize the power we possess to create change, make the world better and alter the lives humans. If you think about how our world has grown, changed, evolved and transmuted, the limiting claim of evolution alone simply does not explain or account for many realities we all know exist.

For instance, those who doubt there is a force so powerful that it is at the core of our very existence, then let them try to explain away the depth of the word, inspiration. Where does it come from if not from an infinite energy? Does inspiration come from thin air? It is just plucked from some undefinable source we cannot see? Well, yes! It comes from the collective consciousness and the idea, be it a new technology, an invention that can change the world or just a solution to a problem comes from a brilliant thought wave that is vibrating about looking for its recipient or the seeker in harmony with it whom it can inspire. Understanding that our etheric thought field is always interconnected to the Field, requires that we remain vigilant and stay in a state of constant awareness of that connection and the responsibility that carries.

We affect the future, the present, and possibility with every thought. We have great power when we have great will for will is what projects our thought into the field. Thus, in times of turmoil, angst, upheaval, and the confusion that can arise in those states, it is of the utmost importance we do not project anything into the field. From a psychological perspective, projection is valueless and yet, introspection, looking inward for the cause, is when we draw from the field. We calmly become the patient of the collective consciousness that has the answer we need to gather our wits and move forward once again. We take responsibility for our own growth, and we take responsibility for what we 'Put Out There' that can never be taken back.

Mentalism is the harmonious action of the three most powerful faculties of mental organization, i.e., thought, etheric energy and will.

? Thought is the intelligence collected by the brain, for the use of the mind, from passing vibrations which are in harmony with it.

? Etheric energy is the force generated by the brain by the process of thinking.

? The will is the operator or director and dispatcher, and the will guides the thoughts to their respective stations (recipients)."

The Etheric energy system delivers energy to your physical body so that it can do everything that it does to enable you to generate your life experiences. The Etheric energy system is connected to the emotional energy system and the mental energy system. The energy bodies are integrated, and they speak to one another all the time. Just try to suck the thought back and retrieve it before it has done damage or has presented something to the consciousness that you do not wish to create.

Again, remember, it is okay! Your journey has many steps.

Some will feel like you have stepped backward. Just begin again!

Reading this book requires, at times, you just stop and contemplate what you do not understand because to fully absorb what is being presented requires a shift in consciousness and you must allow your mind time to fully absorb what it means to you. Also, you may experience a bit of anxiety and nervousness. This is exactly what this book is apt to do to everyone because the energy of change is creating the feeling so, breathe, take a break, relax and ride it out in the knowledge that this is exactly the results you are seeking. You will be much stronger and more powerful with each experience. That is good news!

Fortunately, the truth will be revealed to you in a manner you can understand and absorb. I hope you are one of those exceedingly brilliant people who just 'Gets It', but if you are like me, it will take time and thought. Use your mind to consider what is being offered to healers in this book and the more you do, the more you will be using the theory of mentalism. I want to point out that mentalism speaks of creating with thought or imagination. Mentalism will become clearer to you in this book as you focus on the references to the word *mind* when you come across it on the following pages.

Knowledge often makes us uncomfortable because to learn something new usually requires change. Most people resist change simply because that is our limited human nature. Strive to be a person who embraces change with open arms because, I can guarantee you higher beings have higher intellects and they want us to be, dare I say, a little less human? They hope to make us more like them. I relish the thought!

Furthermore, whenever you begin to feel overwhelmed, please consider this individualized truth... Acceptance of the reality of such a fountain of information is all you need to begin to explore it. You can be as any explorer of years gone by and begin to strike out on your own. You can sail through uncharted waters and hike over mountains unseen or undiscovered by anyone else as you begin the journey of learning deeper and more powerful principles of healing selected specifically for you. The route you take will be, as it should be, personalized and individuated to you and you alone. There is no set path to walk. But there are tenants that you must adhere to if you wish to maintain the powers of mentalism you attain.

There are laws of ethics and principles that will help you alter your behaviors and habits of thinking contrary to higher thought and vibration. You may want to write these down and read them every morning before you head off to work or out into a world that does not understand how the universe works. These laws when practiced will also become your protection from harmful energies that try to ensnare you into darkness and low vibrations that will hold you back.

These laws will indeed test your metal and commitment to living in a higher density.

The Laws of Mentalism:

- *I will never yield to temper or entertain irritation*
- *I will never a make a decision in haste*
- *I will never entertain regret after I have made a decision*
- *I will make my decision final and never do anything by halves*
- *I will never act contrary to my own judgement*
- *I will never decide to do that which will injure another*
- *I will always be honest with myself and my dealings with others*
- *I will impress the decisions upon my mind and live up to them every day*

Chapter Four: Continue on Your Journey

Practicing the Laws will make them a reality in your life!

So, develop an understanding of the universes and the Creator of All that Is and once you are comfortable with it, from this vantage point, find your place amongst the brilliance and wisdom that exists there. Assuming you already know how you perceive the universes, the heavens, angelic beings, guides and All that Is, all I put forth today is that you begin to take that into your heart and mind as your Divine Physician and your healing circle, so you can take it with you whenever you conduct a healing session. Delving deeply into the All of etheric thought means you should and can ask questions, expecting the answers to be forthcoming. It is the nature of mentalism...it is divine communication. It is a realm of logic that surpasses all we know as humans because we do not yet completely understand the All and how everything is formulated into a perfected plan for all time, including the future.

Imagine this! The depth of knowledge available is limitless. So, ask away and wait for the answer. Then ask again, always listening in your mind for the response. I have not foolishly assumed that the Law of Mentalism and the Collective Consciousness is being presented in the book as something new...no, instead it is being brought to remembrance. We know this innately and yet the path of finding our purpose and place is that we have to learn it again and remember it in this lifetime and then grow with it. Beyond that and what is important is that we have been changed by evolution, and as such, we are more powerful in conducting and receiving this energy source than ever before.

Remember! We will continue to grow in our creative capabilities and healing power as we surround ourselves with its dynamic current and flow and learn how to conduct it by speed, intensity etc. Amazing! And of supreme responsibility when you consider the impact, negative positive we may have. As we move together through the book it will become obvious that the techniques we will be taught to use to magnify and focus the energetic patterns and fields that are available the more it will become apparent the oldest form of healing (energetic) is still in existence because it is inextricably connected to humans and is the most natural source of natural healing ever. It is from our origins or Source, and it is spiritual healing.

The focus of the new energy is to expand our understanding that via Mentalism or thought that we understand that all healing is spiritual. We adhere to the principles of holism and the holistic approach to healing. And yet, what we must grasp is that the order of mind, body, spirit healing must shift to Spirit, Mind and then Body. For without a sound spiritual foundation and high spiritual vibration in succinct identifiable patterns of energetic flow, one cannot be healthy in the body or mind. Spirit or mind is the life source. If the mind is run amuck with stressors, worry, chaos and illness then such is merely a symptom of a depleted spirit connection. If the body is weak and failing, it is merely a symptom of a depleted spirit.

~Spirit is the life force and if it is not being nurtured, it will shrivel and die and leave the body for greener pastures, so to speak. If the spirit is well fed, nurtured, allowed to vibrate with radiant life energy it will indeed nurture the body to keep it well if the spirit chooses to reside in that form or bit of matter. Spirit requires mobility, serenity, solemnity, all quiet attributes and yet there is no stillness in a spirit that is vibrating rapidly and powerfully. Thus, it seems a bit of a paradox does it not? People meditate to quiet the mind, reduce stress and allow the spirit to connect with or touch the divine. It is very powerful to reduce the stress felt by the physical body and yet the spirit prefers a bit of action, mobility, flow and ebb, and power. Like plugging a lamp into an outlet, the light generated by high voltage electromagnetic energy will build the spirit rapidly and fully and it will become luminous with power to sustain it. If spirituality is sustained, the body and mind will reflect that perfect state in perfect wellness. That is why shamans dance, sing, chant, move, shout and make music. It feeds the spirit.

Similarly, native tribes sing, dance with great energy and speed and sing during ceremony. Some churches have vivacious services with powerful choirs and rhythmic music. All such activities feed the spirit if the intent is to connect to spiritual energy and Source. Drumming and rhythm create a frequency as well and the higher the vibration the higher the frequency rises in the energetic field of the shaman. The resultant trance like state can be initiated by the density of the spiritual field of the shaman and when its density matches that of another dimension then communication and telepathy become simplified.

There within that dimension one encounters the healers who are waiting to assist and teach. Please consider this unusual method I was shown as another example of the same technique, but it was easier, quicker and required only intention and spiritual presence.

By spiritual presence I mean that my spirit was attuned to the event, not my mind nor my body. It was energy at work and intention that brought about the fruition of my spirit rising from an obvious and annoying slump! Upon waking one summer morning I felt like a sloth. I was moving without intention, wandering about aimlessly and despite my slump, I was oddly anxious. I had not been resting well for a few nights and was also tired from physical work. Inquiring of my guides and healing angels, the answer that came was like a lesson or class in raising my vibration with ease.

It began with a shower. While I was washing, I kept following instructions as they came. I scrubbed with a washcloth without soap. I then scrubbed with a cloth and soap and deliberately acknowledged how much better the smooth strokes of the slippery soap felt. Next, I moved my hands with intentions of sweeping away negative energy from my body by beginning at my head, swirling my hands around then sweeping down across my body and shaking off the negativity. As I rinsed under the soothing life-giving water, I watched the water graciously rinse away my angst and worry. It did so without complaint or hesitation. While watching the movement of the water as it swirled down the drain I heard, "See the water. It moves fearlessly to its destination even though it knows not where it goes or what will happen along the way. It simply flows! You can do anything you want to water, and it will find a way to restore itself. You can even defecate in it and it will rejuvenate and cleanse itself. It just does not respond. Be the water, Lana, be the water. Go wherever life takes you and do not react to anything or anybody. *Just go with the flow.*"

As I watched the water go down the drain, I thanked it for washing away the debris I had been accumulating. It looked lovely and peaceful as it moved. Next, after drying I got a glass of energized water and placed in on my dresser. I used my hands to instill a very high frequency into the small glass of crystal-clear water. Then, finding the next step quite unusual, I took a moment to focus and then pushed my spirit field out of my body and into the tiny glass. Then with my hand, I replicated a small vortex action above the water and pulled my cleansed and energized spirit from the water and breathed it back into my body. I felt amazingly clean, refreshed, and totally alive. I moved with restored purpose and my mind was clear to focus on my day and plans for action and duties. I was quite astounded by the whole process. It was complete!

Now, when I feel stressed or annoyed, I simply remind myself...Be the water Lana, just be the water and go with the flow for this moment. Be the water and not care about that which does not matter." It sets me right very quickly and I can move on. I was most thankful for the class in cleansing and the greater appreciation I gained for water. I began to imagine its path through sewers and drainpipes to connect with rivers and eventually the ocean. I thought of its lack of hesitancy to just keep moving through and around any obstacle in its path. Through it all water seems to have no reaction, only action. Even after all the ways in which we abuse and use water with little to no respect, it continues to grant us life. It cleanses away debris and dirt from the surface of everything it touches. It is so powerful in its adaptable form; so lovely in its fluidity and willingness to change.

Be the water! It is good to remind yourself that alternatives to stress do exist! The more you remind yourself, the more you will automatically go with the flow and do it with grace.

Walk with Wisdom

It is relevant that classes such as this one just shared are moments of elucidation and education that we are all capable of experiencing on a regular basis. The higher we raise our vibration by being a student of higher beings, the more likely we are to be offered more classes that can increase our chances of moving yet higher again. Wisdom is never to be overrated. Wisdom is the greatest gift, and it is what the Sage is noted for. Wisdom is what we need, and we can never get enough of it. That is evidenced by all the lessons we still have to learn, in this life and ones that follow.

Thus, to learn to 'Be the Water' is done with the full awareness of the flow of life and where it and we are in the full circle of life. We can stay in the present in a state of astounding peace of mind, we can avoid the drama of ego and shelter our precious spirits from the pain and separation the world is still healing. And we can help it heal by always sending loving thoughts into the collective consciousness so that when a soul is mentally asking, "How do I heal from this?" We can be part of the solution because we are projecting healing loving energy for them to receive. We can be more like the water that cleanses everything it touches and become a very powerful force. The true beauty of this is in knowing that what we are thus sending, is what we are thus receiving. We alone have the power to control what is drawn into our field as recipients.

It seems that the struggle of maintaining a loving attitude is complicated by all that happens around us. We can be surrounded by people and problems that are anything other than uplifting. To remain accepting of the issues of the world in a manner that promotes healing is complex. It is hard not to form judgments about another's behavior. It is difficult to tolerate abuses and actions that reduce our power as people of God. Mainly because healers are empathic. So, we feel the pain the world is enduring, and we wish it to be resolved. Oh, that we could just stop the violence! The world could be a much better place. For all the beauty in this world, it is easy to slip into the doldrums of seeing all the ugliness too and that brings us down.

However, as healers, if we do not see the illness and understand its origins, we cannot heal it. So, we cannot wear blinders and shut ourselves off from it in isolation unless we can affect the world from within such isolation. Which we can do if we have the will to change it. Even from isolation we can usher in shifts in consciousness that enable the vast majority of people to live in peace if we focus intently on the field and implant organic thoughts of purity and love. This is so true of contemporary shamanism.

~Today's Shaman is being summoned to focus upon that which can be done to alter the entire world and raise it ever higher on a global scale. We will be given the gift of the energy required to do it. And we will not be working alone!

Revised Energetic Connections are Obviously Safe

Knowing who we are contacting when communicating telepathically with guides seems less risky than it was even ten years ago. We can surmise that is because we have a higher vibratory field that we are in now, which is due to the shifts that have been taking place. We are coming back around again in our evolutionary phases, much like at the time when the spiritually advanced societies such as Atlantis, Ancient Egyptians, Sun Worshippers, and Mesopotamia existed and as evidenced had contact with beings from other planets or dimensions.

We are being contacted and offered a different type of lifestyle and technological advances that make us look medieval. The higher our own vibration has progressed the less likely we are to contact or attract low vibration or dark entities. Now we are talking to angels and other light beings that come to admonish us that we need to ally with the forces of light and become actively involved in the fracas that is taking place in the universes that surround us. We can help heal our world when we help heal others as well, because all are part of the collective consciousness.

Defining the source of your information is easily attainable because you merely ask who you are talking to and expect to get an answer. Archangels will readily identify themselves by name and ETs, though a bit more hesitant, will let you know details of who they are and oftentimes where they are from. ETs use a different approach than angels and you will come to recognize the difference in the dialogue and how they present themselves. They are not as patient as angels and can be very direct in their approach to logic and truth. They see things quite differently than humans do and will promptly point out the need for peace and living differently than we do in order to preserve and usher in a brighter future for our planet and ourselves. ET's possess elaborate healing techniques and energy, so they are excellent sources of information and healing power. I find them utterly fascinating.

Given that the focus of the information offered in this book centers on mentalism, to illustrate further what I mean about open mental communication, I will tell a little story. Years back, probably the late 1990's, I was reading online about the CSETI (Center for the Study of Extraterrestrial Intelligence) organization. I studied for a moment, the vast satellite dishes they had set up to hear communications from outer space.

I concluded that this was a silly endeavor given I had been communicating with ETs for some time by then and all was done telepathically using just my mind. I would think 'the invitation' in an unknown tongue, one word that means "Greetings" (word not shared for safety's sake) and project my thought words toward the skies when I believed ships were passing by and then, communication would begin.

I would listen to what they desired to share and answer the questions they posed. Over the years of my experiences, I was prompted many times by a spirit guide to go outdoors when some ship was in my vicinity. I would then strike up a conversation. Some were lengthy and others exceedingly brief. Whatever the circumstance, I have always enjoyed talking with them. While I was perusing the CSETI website, I had briefly considered contacting them to suggest the same to them but left well enough alone knowing it would soon become evident.

Now, if you look at CSETI's website today, they are stating, "Contact protocols include the use of light, sound, and thought. Thought - specifically consciousness - is the primary mode of initiating contact." They discovered they could communicate with ET's telepathically."

I was so pleased that somehow, they had found the way and it probably developed at the prompting of those contacting them when their vibrations were high enough. ET's come from so many dimensions within the universe, and they are working to protect us from ourselves and our self-destructive patterns of life. Yes, there are those who are here to steal from us, take our energy, our minerals, and even our water...but those whom I have been contacted by are benevolent because as mentalism works, I connect with those who wish to bring blessings as that is my intent. Like attracts like, in other words.

My intentions reach those who have the same mindset as I do...essentially, my tenant is "Do No Harm," i.e., the same tenant as true healers throughout time. I believe that all of those I have communicated with over the course of all the years I have been doing this type of thing, have become, in some way, part of my healing circle. I can call upon specialists for specific reasons because the circle is large; maybe limitless. This is reassuring to me because healing can be complicated in some cases, and we need all the professional help we can get.

Given you have a healing circle or that you will quickly acquire one, you should never feel alone in your journey or afraid to explore it. You are always accompanied by your spirit guides and unseen beings who are hoping to impart more knowledge to anyone who will listen and use the knowledge to benefit others. I know I am not unique in my skills as a shaman, but I am also aware that because I have been communicating with beings numbering in the hundreds for over three decades, I am confident sharing my knowledge of how it is so important to the effectiveness of a shaman or healer.

What they offer takes us beyond our limitations and expands our knowledge of that which is unseen, not clearly definable and often intangible yet very real energy that can alter and correct our etheric fields to a state of wellness.

Chapter Summary/Key Takeaways

It is different now for good reason!

It is no longer something to fear or approach with skepticism. It is new level of energy that has been building in our dimension since we have become more open to energetic patterns, wavelengths and understanding of how the body functions holistically as energy. We have opened ourselves to the higher truths and have thus raised our minds above the level of mere tangibility of that which we can readily see and touch. It is a new day, because we are willing to think about what remains to be discovered within the power of our minds. Furthermore, as light workers have grown in their understanding of universal truths, they have broadened the scope of the collective consciousness to include that which is obtainable to the spiritually minded seeker.

Angelic Interpretation of Healing

This heightened awareness has moved us far beyond the ancient texts we have relied upon for thousands of years. We have shifted our dimensional thought out of the 3rd dimension into the higher density of thought I believe to be the 5th dimension (or density as some now define it) and of the ability to reach for the stars, grasp 58 them and feel them vibrate within our hands. With that said to reassure you, what I was recently offered to share entails some specific details to consider when exploring the mental aspects entailed in healing. Let me elaborate now...This was offered in outline from by Archangel Raphael after he asked me to write this book.

The topics are as follows:

1. All healing is created by thought
2. All healing is projected from your mind
3. All healing is incidental
4. All healing is incremental
5. All healing is natural

Explained:

Number 'One All Healing is Created by Thought'

The statement, 'All healing is created by thought' can be further explained as intentional or setting an intention however, deeper understanding includes the awareness that guidance from healing masters will be offered as to what steps to take and what energies to project and where to project them during the healing session. It is a time of listening thoughtfully and following the advice you are offered while you are conducting energy. This premise is why we must learn more about mentalism and connecting telepathically to the universal thought energy.

"Healing is created by thought" also simply means that, as above, so below. Your thought will project you above to connect to teachers and the result will be evident below or where you are at the moment. It is further understood as your engaging your mind's connection with a higher vibration which enables your body to conduct the energy flow or wave that is made evident. You will 'see it' so to speak in your mind and in seeing the waves of energy and how they are intended to perform you can thus cooperate with them as they instruct where to move, shift and intensify the frequency.

You have become the conductor, in other words. Furthermore, if you use traditional methods of antiquity, you will burn sage, clear the negative energy that is present and then place hands, crystals, wands or what have you over the affected area. However effective that has been for you, now you can learn to conduct energy that is of a much higher vibration than known to you previously. This includes Reiki practioners too who have not all traditionally used fetishes but use their hands as instruments. For example, I stopped burning sage many years ago when I was warned it was insufficient to the task. Practice as you choose of course!

Now, I use my hands and intent to clear away stagnant or negative energy by sweeping it away with energy patterns and colors that are powerful enough to do a thorough cleaning. In such higher vibrational energy modes, healing becomes more focused and intentional because it is with a direct and less indirect purpose. You have the expertise of Perfect Healers like the Archangel Raphael and those whom he has taught to impart knowledge to less enlightened beings like us. The guess work of hopeful intention setting is thus negated because you 'just know' you are doing the right thing at the right time.

See why it is an imperative to sharpen your ability to hear and follow instructions?

Number Two 'All Healing is Projected from Your Mind.'

Imagine you are connected, you are hearing and seeing what is being offered as a healing plan, energy, model, and program. You have seen or heard your instruction so now, using your mind alone you project that same energy through your hands into your client. Focus is required, and you maintain that current until told to do otherwise. You may move your hands in a different direction or position, but the energy will/must continue to flow where it is supposed to go. You will move it with your mind by telling it what to do.

If you are truly opened mentally, you can simply feel the energy move into the person you are working for and let the experts conduct the flow for you while you act as a conduit. Trust is required, and this method is what you are aiming for. Many may dismiss this idea as old news, but please be advised that once you have read this book the power of your healing energy will increase exponentially. We are bringing a new more powerful energy into fruition and action as Today's Shamans!

Number Three 'All healing is incidental'

(def. liable to happen as a consequence of an activity) means healing is directly related to how closely you follow directions, can hear instructions and trust in what you are guided to do. Healing accompanies your ability to deliver the right frequency at the right time. The right frequency is directly proportioned to your connection with a healing master or masters. It also means that the right type of activity will by consequence effect a more accurate outcome or more effective healing than the wrong type or inadequate type of activity. Sound a bit scary and maybe carries too much responsibility? No...you just need to be open and trust that the right energy is being offered and let it flow. You can trust your guidance if you have established a strong connection to healers like Raphael and specialists who can address your client's most pressing need.

For example, if you have a client that has heart trouble, you need to summon a heart specialist and make that need known when you connect to the source of healers present at the time. Then, knowing you have a specialist assisting in your healing increases your confidence, your power, and the outcome, which is by consequence now more specific to the needs of the body you are healing.

Number Four: 'All Healing is Incremental.'

This is self-explanatory because we all know that healing takes time just because that is the way our bodies work. Even miraculous healing will come with the necessity of time required by the body and mind to adjust. For example, a person who nearly drowns and is saved by resuscitation will bear witness, in many instances, that by all rights they should not have survived. Even when divine intervention spares them, their bodies will reflect a shocked effect, some tissue damage, and in time will return to normal, but cellular, nervous system and emotional healing takes time. It may be shortened in some instances, but just the awareness that it takes time alleviates the risk of relying upon visible signs of healing immediately. Often, even 24 hours can make a big difference in how the client feels. Patience is necessary, in other words, and trust is imperative.

Imagine if you received healing from someone and you just knew that you were healed. Even the state of awe you would be in will take some time of introspection, appreciation, gratitude, and understanding the aspects of how that healing will affect your future spirituality and life. Divine healing will indeed have an impact on your spirituality and life and both concepts would deserve some attention. That new awareness too will become apparent in increments, so you can fully absorb your new wisdom.

*You will need to advise your clients about those facts, so they remember to express gratitude and open their hearts to the spiritual changes that will follow...maybe for days or months. They will certainly feel different having experienced a much higher vibration than their bodies and minds are accustomed to.

Number Five "All Healing is Natural".

Certainly, you are aware of this fact and yet when you really look at it stated in such a manner, it creates a deeper knowing. Consider, not only does our body heal naturally, it is also natural to heal. Our bodies are designed to heal and do so very efficiently if we give the body what it requires to do so. Now, consider how completely natural energetic healing is, given that we are energy. Every action and reaction in our world happen energetically. Communication or acquisition of knowledge of any kind occurs only with an energy transfer. There are no exceptions. This is a rule of nature.

We must consider that if energy exchange is obviously that pervasive in nature that it must naturally be that pervasive in our bodies as well. So, understanding how it can be manipulated to promote healing is well worth the pursuit. Wouldn't you agree? It is no secret that an area of the body that is sickened is suffering from a very low energy flow. During a healing session, you will be offered a high frequency energy vibrational pattern that will raise the vibration of the same area to a healthy frequency. It will indeed be a higher and faster pattern that will by the very nature of holistic principles create a healing environment. To illustrate, picture if you will, an elderly person that is apparently suffering from depleted energy. He or she has a vacant stare from eyes that are opaque looking and lifeless, with slumped shoulders and a slow gait.

If I see a person like that, I want to reach and touch them on the arm, just long enough to create an energy flow that will lift them up. I believe such an exchange is possible, wherein the slightest touch, done with intention can rejuvenate their body. I also believe before too long with knowledge and passion that I will be able to do such a loving act with a great outcome. People crave touch because it recharges them with energy. The sad fact of a life that does not include regular renewal of energy flow by spiritual means reflects the result of a body on low ebb. That image is similar to the appearance of any body, young or old, that needs stronger vibrational patterns of energy. A body that houses a mind that does not connect with the flow of spirit energy, that by its natural function renews strength and vitality, will show signs of depletion and a depleted spirit results in a dying body.

When you think about it...we are spiritual energy so given that the spirit is here to find a higher self, it is not inconceivable that when the spirit is starved for renewal and reconnection with a higher plane of love and an embrace from the heavens that it will not succumb to total depletion. The spirit, by right of eternal existence, will instead allow the body to die so it can return to its origins for renewal and possibly rebirth into a new body that will ensure its chances of finding enlightenment. The spirit, I believe has the same will to survive as the body and it sees the disconnect of a non-spiritual life as a useless life wherein it cannot fulfill its purpose for being here.

In essence then, the will to survive is truly supported because we are after all, spirit and not the body we reside in for a time.

Examine a powerful theory why some people perform and live better than many others.

Being in the flow of the energy of life.[1] YouTube video with the founder of the theory

Living in flow - the secret of happiness with Mihaly Csikszentmihalyi at Happiness & Its Causes 2014

---

1. https://www.youtube.com/watch?v=TzPky5Xe1-s

Chapter Five: Energetic Transmutation

Power comes from Power

Power that we are accustomed to hearing about is similar to the healing power we require but, in this case, it is simply not the same thing. Electromagnetism is the source of our field of energy and yet the new energy you can build and transfer to another is not the same. In essence, this is heightened spiritual power and our bodies are not spirit in that sense. The vibration is heightened or faster because it is not 3rd dimension energy.

Our bodies are comprised of matter and matter is energy condensed to a slow vibration. Matter can deteriorate and decay, (change) but energy cannot be destroyed. So, bear in mind that you are healing organs, cells, tissue etc. which is all matter. Does energy sustain the matter? No, matter sustains matter. Food, water, air, blood, vitamins, minerals and so forth sustain matter. Spirit Energy is contained within the matter or body or encapsulated in a mass of cells and tissue. It is contained like light from a bulb. You can see it and feel its heat but if the bulb is broken the energy dissipates. If a body dies, the spiritual energy dissipates. So, you can see that the two forms of energy, i.e., heightened (fast) spiritual energy and power we are familiar with are vastly different.

The power we are now seeking to find, the heightened spiritual power, comes from the Universal All. It is cumulative and not individualized like our spirit is now here on Earth. This heightened power can be directed but it cannot be contained. Imagine tapping into a universal sized source of power. Awesome! To effectively conduct the powerful new energy that is now being offered you have to be strong enough to endure it. You also must be strong enough to control and direct it. It is easier than we might imagine but it can be a bit exhausting because, to heal in this manner requires a lot of your own material energy. It is possible to control, direct, and conduct the energy with relative ease if you have increased your own power because you will not be altering your energetic pattern as much if it is already more similar to the faster vibrations flowing through you.

This will take place as your connection increases and with time spent absorbing the higher vibrations. Power comes from power!

Build your Power to a Higher Vibration.

You can build your power to a higher vibration gradually and effectively by spending time with the heightened power you will eventually use to heal others. You can connect by thinking about it and asking for the connection to be instilled. Remember, it is all in your mind. Once you have determined that you have a connection then spend time talking and while you are in conversation be mindful of your need to be aware of the energy that surrounds you. Sense it, move it, ask it to move you. You will find that you are changing your own energy level to a higher vibration because you are asking it to be raised. I will offer an exercise to practice raising your vibration but first, let's ensure that you can talk with and hear your guides. If you already have an open line of communication, then you are blessed. If you have been trying to connect, then rest assured that it is easier now than it ever was before. I know many who have regular conversations with their guides and with angels. That was simply not the case even a short decade ago. People tried to meditate to hear them when in fact they needed to raise their vibration, so they could absorb the energetic pattern communication creates. The greatest barrier to being able to hear and communicate openly is one of lack of trust. Many people already hear their spirit guides speaking to them but have become so accustomed to the chatter that they misconstrue the guides voices for that of their own thoughts.

Rarely do people hear in a voice that is different from the sounds of their own voice in their heads. It does happen however but usually only in experienced clairaudients. I am not saying there are not exceptions because we are all on a different path and have different experiences. What I hope to elaborate is that one must trust that when they hear that still small voice, one can trust that they are connected and build that trust by asking questions and waiting for replies. The reply is heard in your thoughts but emanates from a different area of your brain. It is hard to explain but it feels a little less centralized and off in one direction or a bit higher in your brain. A little off to the left if that makes sense! Even the reply will likely sound like your normal thought until you begin receiving answers that you know you did not have the knowledge to supply.

The keys are quietude, isolation from others and an active imagination which can carry you to a place of a heightened awareness of what is going on in your mind. It is not unlike meditation and yet it does not normally create deep relaxation. It can be invigorating and unsettling as you move through the teaching and your question-and-answer scenario. Asking question after question and getting the reply is what you are striving for and trusting the reply as sourced from your guides is what you must focus upon. If you have never tried to communicate openly before, then let your guides know that you need their help in establishing an open line of communication and envision a cord going out from your mind that stretches into other dimensions just outside your body and wait for someone to answer the call you have made.

Do not try to reach way out into the universe because the 4th and higher dimensions are no higher than that of tall trees. You are already always moving within higher dimensions; you are just not fully aware of them. Create a comfortable spot to lie down. In the area of about 2 feet above your head, place a large clear quartz crystal. This is the spot that your Soul Star Chakra is located above you. It is inside your auric field but in most cases, it has never been activated. It is not the same as your crown chakra but will work with your crown chakra. It is one more than a dozen chakras or power points we are not accustomed to using or even activating. Some are below our feet and the rest above our heads.

Now, lying on your back in a comfortable spot, you should place your hands (Left hand over the Right hand) just below your sternum. First, strive to create energy flowing through your hands until you feel obvious warmth and a good degree of vibration in your hands. Think of this as an energetic connection. Therefore, the more energy you can feel in your hands, the greater are your chances of connection. If you feel totally blocked and nothing is happening, then call upon the Archangel Michael to clear any blocks and ask him to cut any cords that hold you connected to the 3rd dimension. Some have more cords than normal which hold their astral body closely attached to their physical body that connects the physical body to the etheric body, onwards to the astral body and finally to the mental body. [They are silver cords that emerge from your back so you may feel sensations there. It may seem strange to ask them to be loosed but, in many instances, they are simply holding one too tight to allow that one to project themselves out of the body to any degree.

If you are afraid and doubtful, ask that you be reassured of your safety by a feeling of warmth throughout your body. Ask them to help you in any way possible to connect you with your guides or any angels present. Like your mind, your vision is actively engaged with your eyes closed because you are watching for color changes, fields of light patterns and anything out of the ordinary. It seems a bit strange but looking off to the left of your peripheral vision will hasten your connection. We strive to move upward naturally because of our years of training that God is above 'out there somewhere' but now we are learning that the ether and the majesty it contains is so much closer than we ever imagined. In fact, moving to the left of your energy field is the easiest way for a shaman to shift into another dimension when doing soul retrieval or searching for a fragment of a person who is dissipated and wanting in life energy.

Do not rush the process because it can take some time for your etheric field to make the changes necessary to accommodate the energy of higher beings. The shifts can make you uncomfortable and the feeling can last for hours, even days. Set aside plenty of time and use an eye mask to block out any light so you can see deeply into the darkness. Be advised that you may have strange sensations in your eyes after you have connected. Your sight may be blurry for a bit, and you may experience eye discomfort. It will pass. If you need to simply lie down for a bit in a darkened room with your eyes resting.

If you are adventurous, you can lie in a totally darkened room and look into the blackness surrounding you with your eyes open. You may see energy patterns approaching you, touching you, and even healing you so you can connect. Do not be deterred if you see some strange things, because you very well may. If you become afraid, let your guides know you need more reassurance. Your emotions can run high on your voyages into the unknown because the loving energy you will encounter can move you to tears of joy. You may feel totally engulfed in a loving embrace that will overwhelm you with emotions and because love is the pervasive energy you will feel less afraid of the unknown. I write as if I am speaking solely to novices who have never experienced this type of event and so if I am overstating the results, please understand such is for the benefit of the novice and not the seasoned traveler with strong telepathic powers.

Do the Work

Thus, for the novice...when you feel the time is right or you hear a voice, begin asking questions and wait for a reply. If you feel you only imagined it...remember, imagination plays a vital role in your ability to hear. If you find it impossible to hear a reply, then start with simple questions like asking the name of the one you have contacted. The names are most often common names like Bill or Dan so if you hear names like that it is alright. Take note of the name offered and say, "I am pleased to meet you." Introduce yourself and then begin again with simple questions. It is always helpful to ask, "What do I most need to know today?"

Because that question is vague, you will not know what to expect as an answer, thus it is easier to trust in the answer you receive as from someone other than yourself. It really is quite simple because your guides will do everything they can to help you. You may hear sounds in your house that you are not familiar with like banging or thumping and that would be your guides or angels who are actively seeking your ack acknowledgment that they are present. Some hear doors open and shut and they note that their pets hear and see things too.

Now, with each contact you build the power that surrounds you by asking them, telepathically remember, to increase the energy flow to an even higher level. It is all done with your mind in open communication and thought. It is not meditation because you must get your mind actively engaged in conversation. You can imagine you have picked up the phone and said, "Hello". You may not know who is on the other end but just knowing from experience that the phone works, trust that someone is on the other end waiting for your call. Do this each time you connect. Let the higher vibrational power be the judge of what you can sustain and allow your guides to control the amount of energy you receive.

You will know when you are done with a session. This may take weeks so, do not be in any hurry. Then, you could conceivably make this a lifelong practice because the energy you are connecting to is limitless and there will be times throughout your life that you need answers to specific questions. Remember to ask! The level you wish to receive is left entirely up to you. If you feel prepared to receive more on an ongoing basis, then do so. It does not require any special preparation like drumming to get in a trance state or burning special incense unless that is something important to you. This is the new day of the shaman and all you need is your mind and your ability to connect in conversation.

Do not make it harder than it needs to be and please do not give up if it takes a few attempts. Given that this book is inspired by Raphael, the words on the pages will become your new reality. Many things have a natural higher vibration, and this book is one. It is inspired, it is guided and edited by the Archangel Raphael. It contains the higher energy of his words and his action. Do not rush the reading of it and always look for messages that are meant specifically for you. What seems to jump out at you will be a boost of energy for you to speed you along your way to being part of a movement that is being created now.

Believe in yourself and your helper spirits. If you know how to communicate openly already then please, for the sake others, take a moment to say a prayer for those still struggling to connect openly with their guides. At any time in your reading of this material connect with Raphael and Gabriel and ask for their assistance and guidance. Also, be sure your guides are engaged too and coordinating everything they can help with. They will love to be involved. This particular exercise should be used to intentionally and physically to raise your vibration any time you need it and particularly before a healing session.

Sit in a comfortable position. Hold out both hands palm up. Now imagine energy forming in your hands until it feels like they will not close. The healing energy is circular in motion so transform it to a tall cylinder of energy that you bring down around your body. Then flatten it into a disc that you move under your body. Then resting on it...lift it and you up to a higher density and vibration. You intend that you have just shifted to the 5th dimension, which you indeed have. Now root yourself there by sending silver cords down into the plane beneath you and attach your cords to the white light there.

Now: Some specifics to remember so you can maintain the power you are to receive are listed here: Be honest in all things. True healing cannot come from one who does not own their own healing. Deception of any sort will destroy your power. There are no shortcuts in this endeavor, and you must live a life with a pure heart. "And in me there shall be no lie."

This is your credo. Be honest in all things. Take good care of yourself and do what is best for you. You need to assert your will over those things of this world that are not in your best interest. It can be bad habits, a poor diet, a life of negative emotions or just despair. Despair has no place in a healer's life because it robs you of your power. Balance in all things can keep you in the right frame of mind and allow you to be present in the now.

Now I offer a message from Raphael the Great Healer

Quote from Raphael

"A true healer of the magnitude we are seeking has little to no emotion. The emotion we are referring to is that which is not an expression of joy. Anger, sullenness, depression, fear, and other such emotional reactions are not coming from a place of joy. To control your emotions is easy if you are using an energetic connection that comes from a higher vibration. When you are vibrating rapidly you will not react to the things you normally do react to at a slower vibration. You will see things with your mind and not with your heart. Trust is the key and here is why!

The more time you spend in the higher vibration the more you will become a thinker and not so much a doer. In other words, you will spend so much time thinking and communicating telepathically with entities that will become your dearest friends that you will not have the desire to react. You will then be thinking at a higher vibration as well. This is the most amazing aspect of the life we are offering you if you can accept it as a real possibility. Let me make it clear that to be free of emotion is what separates us from you. We are higher beings because we use our minds to the fullest extent to create and engage in very worthwhile endeavors. We do not waste precious energy on nonsense or things that take away our energy.

Have you ever had an experience with a guide or angel wherein that entity had an emotional response to your questions, agitation, doubts, queries that are not appropriate, such as anger or impatience? No, of course you have not! Emotions like fear are not within us because we see the whole picture, the future, and we see the reason for your discomfort, so we do not react. Think of a person you know that does not seem to get angry or does not react to stress with a negative response. They just seem to go on about their day as usual and do not get riled up about anything. This is a stable person. Their energy is powerful and stable.

It does not mean they do not feel anything. Quite the contrary. They feel happy most of the time. They are referred to as loving and accepting. They are great people to be around. Contrarily, instability is reflective of something gone wrong. Angry people are not the type anyone wants to be near because they rob of you of your happy feeling. They steal your energy, in other words. They steal because they need it to exist, literally. Volatile people are on edge all the time and nearly ready to explode or implode because they are desperate to steal energy to live. Actions speak louder than words and if a person is tense, irritable, crabby all the time or just plain mean spirited, they are at an extremely low ebb energetically and...they are afraid. They sense their weakness (spiritual weakness) and know they are dying.

My point is this; understand that energy or the lack thereof in this plane is indicative of a person's spiritual power. Power is apparent when a person is healed, and healing is apparent when a person has power. The more power a person has the more health they will exhibit. That, my dears, is simple logic. There are as many variations of this theme as there are people in the world and not all people are the same, of course, but there are simple rules that apply too.

Generally, people are pretty much the same. They react to the same stimuli in the same ways. What you must be on the watch for are the extremists. Anyone can have a bad day due to exhaustion, fatigue, grief, and stress. They will rest and recover. It is those that never change their stripes that you need to really try to understand because if you can understand them, you can understand why you do not want to be like them and can prevent that from happening. Understanding is followed logically by empathy. Empathy is followed logically by an expression of love and kindness. So, contemplate this! Those on the highest vibrational plane understand, so they do not react. And they understand because they are on a higher vibrational plane. They understand because they were once at a lower vibration like humans and now, they are more like those on a faster vibration.

This would be your goal in this group; to be more like them. Emotions are ruled by hormones and hormonal responses. Hormones are controlled by the brain and the brain is controlled by thought. If thoughts are not projected toward an emotion, then emotions will not rule the individual. You might be wondering how this book headed off in the direction it has taken. Well, according to the theory of mentalism as attributed to Hermes, a person is what he thinks. He has created himself according to the image of the world his mind has created. He will reflect what he thinks the world, or this plane is. What he imagines this world to be will also be reflected in his ability to tap into a higher vibrational energetic plane. If he does not believe, then he cannot connect because in his mind; guides or teachers do not exist. His disbelief negates his ability to connect.

Faith is a funny thing. If you only have a little faith, you will only be able to accept low energy vibrations. The mind receives what the mind perceives. Simply put if you do not believe much you surely cannot receive much. The kicker is, if you believe a little and receive a little, then you believe more and receive more, then you are off and running and can receive, over time, limitless amounts of energy. Many teachers have extolled faith as a way to obtain wealth. You just have to believe in it enough and give enough to receive enough. Scriptures are thus twisted to obscure the real message and that message was originally meant to refer to power. Creating your own existence has been distorted into a materialistic approach to gain.

It was originally intended to mean spiritual energy. Sure, people can in faith, create a material item like money or possessions but that is not the intent of those teachings. Christ knew that to be like him meant you had to have power to do the things he did. He was not, as a pauper, referring to material things or wealth. He meant power. Do you give to receive? Then you have relinquished the gift of power for goods.

When you believe hype, you are instilled with hope. Hope is not faith. It is a wish and a prayer maybe and then the disappointment in failure destroys your faith. It is indeed a modern paradox or contradiction based on just enough truth to ensnare you. This is not at all what Hermes meant. He meant, you will become what you think, and your world will reflect what you perceive it to be. Sometimes there is truth in what you perceive as negative about this world, but that truth can be ignored, disallowed and rendered ineffectual in your life if you rise above it in thoughts that are more like a higher vibration.

In fact, you can physically as well as mentally rise above this dimension if you learn how to adjust your thought in accordance with the higher vibration of the dimension you connect with. It is, like all healing, incremental and your growth comes in steps or stages. Each step or thought that moves you forward will increase the speed at which you will take the next step and the next. You can really move forward swiftly if you are giving your time and thought to thinking on a higher level." Raphael

Love is the Energy that Heals

You will do great things on higher levels naturally because you have built your energy to a higher vibration. The characteristics of loving kindness, empathy, understanding, and compassion are defined as the 'nature of love'. Truly exceptional vibratory patterns exist in the universes that enable one to love unconditionally like Jesus did while here and angels and other entities do on higher planes. Jesus brought peace of mind to those who spent time with him. He was a stable man, or his energy was stabilized at a higher and faster vibration. So, people wanted to be with him. He made them happy. He exuded loving energy and people felt empowered by being near him.

Love is powerful. Being powerful means you come from a place of loving energy that is tangible and can be felt. People certainly felt the healing energy that made the miraculous healings take place when Jesus touched the sick. Keep in mind, he was out of his original higher vibrational setting while he was here. And yet, he still performed miracles. In his teaching he stated we, "Could be like him." He was teaching we could share in that same power. And we can if we can learn to think and act in the manner that Raphael is intending.

Over the years, many healers have developed or came here with this tremendous ability. Here are some examples: Investigate the links below.

Famous Spiritual Healers World's Greatest Healer

World renowned Energy Healer And-In my opinion, the greatest of all energy experts. Legendary physicist Nikola Tesla said, "If you want to find the secrets of the universe, think in terms of energy, frequency, and vibration."

Energy Healer Dean Kraft - The most Scientifically Documented Energy Healer of Our Time (deankrafthealer.com)[2]

Each of these examples will cite in one way or another that they have a circle of healers, angels, guides etc., that direct them while they heal or even take over their bodies to be used as a healing instrument. Amazingly, they have tapped into higher vibrations beginning decades ago. Imagine how significant the energy will be that Raphael keeps clarifying is new. He states, "It will shake the Earth." As a person reading this book, you are being offered a connection to the new earth-shaking changes that are coming. Let that truth sink in...

---

2. http://www.deankrafthealer.com/

Healers come from a place of love.

Love is the energy that heals in that: Love is the Impetus

Compassion for another will move you to heal them. Compassion comes from love and love is an energy. Despite how we view it, love is not an emotion. The simple act of loving another involves an exchange of energy. People are consumed by the need to be loved and to love. People need to be in relationships to be whole. People do not fully understand that love literally feeds more energy into their field. It helps them retain their strength in a world that has a low vibration. For all the needs love meets, it must still be understood as energy. Have you ever noticed that many of our greatest Gurus, healers, spiritualists etc. are single people? Angels do not appear to have mates! That is because they have such a high vibrational energy that they do not need another half to make them whole. Their energy is so strong they can love unconditionally in Spirit. They do not require love to be spiritually whole. They are whole because they are love.

A loving person is a healthier happier individual and they are usually the first to reach out to another in a time of need. They are typically less judgmental and opinionated because they know what truly matters and they ignore trivial things that most people react to. Loving people love life. Love is life energy in its finest form.

Love is the Means

Love has the correct vibration to create healing and wellness. It is a high vibration and in fact, one of the highest frequencies available. What Raphael has conveyed in the discussion about love is that once a healer is vibrating fast and has learned to maintain that frequency, then that healer can use a secret method of healing that is very powerful. Those who will learn to raise their vibration and stay connected to the new healing Circle he has arranged, one will only have to say to their client, "I love you" and the energy sent will be greatly intensified. The chances of healing will be thus greatly magnified.

Raphael is making some amazing promises to those who follow the concepts he is teaching in this book. I can only say, "I am greatly honored he chose me to write the book for him. And I am witnessing firsthand exactly what he means as he brings miracles forth while I am endeavoring to write it." Raphael put it this way: "Many are the ways in which the power will come forward in your life and in all you endeavor to do that is right and true. If you have an honest approach to your choices and always try to do the right thing, even though you may not always be 100% accurate or perfect in your choices and decisions you will be that in a little while, you will be.

Do not subscribe anymore to the saying, "If it sounds too good to be true, it probably is." Those days are gone if you can trust and believe what is being offered to you today, as you read this, whatever day that is. If this book has come into your hands, then you can trust you are meant to have it. And the promises therein are indeed meant for you. If you think that is a pitch to draw you in, if that is a fabrication or manipulation of the truth, then stop reading right now, close this book and walk away because we know you are not who we are looking for. Those who are chosen, will know this is true and will in all graciousness accept the promises herein. They will feel its power.

Now, if someone loves you, really loves you, do they lie to you and deceive you? Certainly not! If you love someone, truly love someone, do you lie to them and deceive them? Certainly not! This is how healing works. It is based on a loving energy that would in no way ever harm or deceive another. We do not have it within us to lie. Why, because we are pure loving energy! There is no harm in us." Maybe, coursing through your veins right now is an energy you are unfamiliar with. Do you feel edgy, fidgety, anxious, and exhilarated all at the same time? Are you on a bit of a spiritual high? Then high five to you because you are open to receive what the new energy offers. Have you ever felt like the world passed you by and you now recognize you have been discovered for the talents you possess?

Welcome to the new world of Today's Shaman! Are there ways in which a select few are called or many are called, few are chosen? Is that biblical verse applicable today? Yes, and this is just the beginning."

My thoughts interjected:

I am reminded of my beginnings many years ago, when it was called the Baptism in Fire by a couple by the name of Charles and Francis Hunter. They were those who sparked a fire in my soul and spiritual being, ignited my life, and blew the embers into flames. I knew, I just knew, I was different from others, and I was trying so ardently to find why that mattered. Mattered, is the crux of the message here.

(Return to Automatic writing with Raphael)

If you are reading this book, you know you want to know why your experiences have mattered. Right? Then yes, you matter, but now we have flipped mattered, to replace purpose, in your case anyway. You have likely felt driven all your days to find what is important, pure, right, just, and significant. Unfortunately, some think the ceremonial process of indoctrination into a sect or religion is significant. It is a membership to a collective yes, but insufficient to bring you to your individual maturity as a healer. A calling? Now that is significant! Those who are called are leaders. Others can be derailed into being followers. They can become ships lost in the night at sea.

Whose shores do you want to stand on at the end of the day? Whose lips do you want to whisper to you the secrets of the universe? Will you pick scientists or spiritualists? Will you seek the divine or will you seek yourself? How do you know that yourself is not divine? In light of the new energy, we can be much more entuned to what we all need to know if we are listening. Are we now listening to some divine source that can really show us the way to righteousness or enlightenment? Or plain and simple, have we finally arrived? Have you felt frustrated and impatient? Do you sincerely wonder if you are on the right path? Have you felt alone, abandoned, ignored and overlooked? Have you been waiting for something marvelously miraculous to come to you? Then you are indeed the one we are looking for. You have been on hold my friend.

You have been on hold, but you have never been forgotten. It is time now.

An Urgency

In the universe that surrounds us, a war is brewing. It will be one of unseen proportions and will affect millions of people and billions of other beings from the galaxies. We need ambassadors of peace and unity, and we beseech you to join our ranks. We desire the strongest warriors from past lives to regain your spiritual oneness and strength and begin to do battle with us once again. If you have found this book, then you were told long ago to come here and wait for this day. You know you are a warrior at heart. You know that you are unlike many others around you. You also know that you are powerful.

At some time in the past, you may have been asked to do battle with darkness and impure things like energy fields that inhabit places of darkness. You have been waiting for your tools and your armor. Do you know how powerful you are? Have you had experiences like commanding the elements? Do you control the wind, fire, water, and air? If you have not, then know that you will. If you raise your hand and thrust it forward, can you feel that you have created an energy shift or displacement. Do you possess the powerful hands of a healer?

These are difficult questions to answer if you do not believe in yourself and have not yet experienced your true power! So, read the words again if you need to and then answer the questions in a positive vein and accept your gifts that are and have been offered. There exists a bit of a time crunch and we need those who are chosen to step forth and volunteer for the mission we are formulating. The plans have been in the works for quite some time now and the time is now to move forward. Do you want us to show you the plan? We can do that as soon as you are ready to hear it.

Such a movement has not been attempted before using humans and yet humans are required as an integral link to all other beings who will be indoctrinated into service. Your world needs you. You need to be part of this movement in order to fulfill your goals and purpose. You have been positioned or stationed in integral locations across the planet. Now you can come together in spirit and in unity to affect great changes for all mankind. If you have an inkling, as many of you do, of what you are asked to do then you know it involves healing. But this healing is of another dimensional pattern heretofore not offered to earthlings. It is used by the most adept healers who heal others who are to be healers in the future. Some will be babies, some will be adults and others will seem most unlikely and yet, healing will ensue.

Energetic medicine is coming in droves to those who understand how the tools can be used and some will find that energetic medicine tools allow for more focused energy patterns and light work. You will no longer feel inadequate to do what you want to do as a healer. You can bring healing energy that can correct distorted fields that cause disruptions in another's pattern. Think of this as brain energy. Imagine the billions of neurons that fire in your brain and magnify your thought processes by 100. The result is energy magnified a hundred-fold. You will heal with thought. You will heal with imagination and mental images of perfection within the body of your clients.

~*" The true sign of intelligence is not knowledge, but imagination."*
-Albert Einstein

Eventually, you will create your own medicine with your hands by adding frequencies to water and alcohol. You will be a driving force in the healing world. Sound interesting? Then stay on task for we are about to begin to provide you with all the energy you need to be a truly dynamic and loving healer. Think of the possibilities and pay attention to all possibilities presented to you. Write them down and store them safely.

Now, rest a moment and utter words of thanks and be pleased that you are on your way, finally on your way.

~" Take rest; a field that has rested gives forth a beautiful crop." -Ovid

PART III: Energy in its Various Forms

The Power of Thought

When you have unequivocally accepted that you are a chosen one, then and only then, can you begin to move forward on the healer's path put before you. There can be no ifs, ands or buts in your private mental conversations with your spirit. You must know that power comes whenever it is summoned and that you do not have to ascertain whether or not the healing will follow. It is the desire of all loving celestial saints to provide healing to an ailing body that deserves to be free from illness and despair.

The energy will be present and yet factors present in the mindset of the sick person, self-care, commitment to healing and the severity of the illness will also contribute to the outcome. One of the biggest barriers to healing a person is the drama associated with the illness and the attention it garners the sick person. This is a hurdle for any in the field of psychology and it spills over into the realm of natural or energetic healing with far too much frequency to be ignored. It is as if the illness grants the person the attention they are not getting otherwise or in some cases, the person could never get enough to be satisfied. Thus, how can you expect them to heal what keeps them feeling appreciated or valued by others they are getting energy from to stay alive. It is like a rock and a hard place for the person who is feeling devalued. They want to be well but if they have nothing to talk about, i.e., their pain and misery, then people will not pay attention to them. That aloneness may be more painful to bear than the illness, so they opt to keep the illness.

Far too many people fit into the needy category because they have never learned to be self-reliant and autonomous. They depend upon others instead for their emotional needs. This book on mentalism is about the power of the mind/spirit, not the brain/body. The new shaman understands that to assist one in healing, the healer must help the weakened person find new strength through the spiritual/energetic approach. As enormous as the task may seem, it is with energy that the transformation begins, and it is with energy that it continues the work of healing the person who has too little confidence to bolster the self from an energetically depleted condition.

More specifically if the person has, let's say, diabetes. We know their pancreas is malfunctioning. Since everything is energy one can assume that the pancreas is not at an optimal point in its frequency. Frequency is indicated by the length of the wave. It is possible that an irregular energetic wave may be visible using an energetic analysis device such as the one I utilize. It is called the VoiceBio Analysis. The client's voice is analyzed for frequencies in waves or notes of music. The amount of energy in each organ is displayed on a screen and the notes that are the lowest are addressed with a myriad of natural treatments.

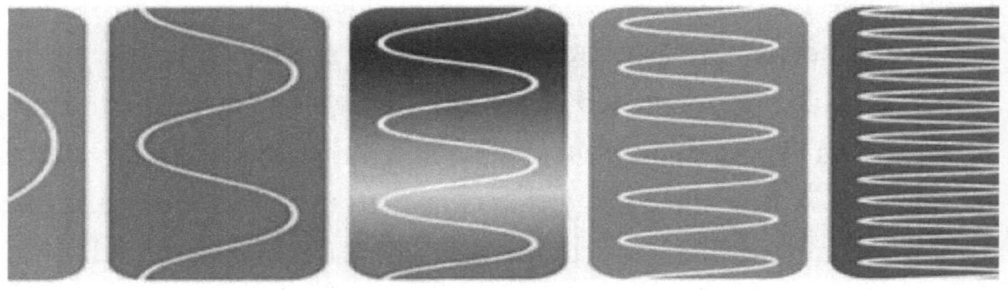

Energy Waves Lowest to Highest Frequency

Energetic devices are more common than ever before. Plus, the VoiceBio gives a practioners the closest thing we have to a diagnostic device. It is actually an assessment tool that provides more exacting energy applications from sound, color and vibration that repairs the organs to optimal energetic frequency. Explaining the device is complex but as an example of what it will reveal is that the liver resonates to the note of G. Thus, applying musical vibrations in that note, will allow the liver to heal. Twelve systems in the body are enhanced with the corresponding note which will bring the body back into harmony with the right frequencies that will promote balance.

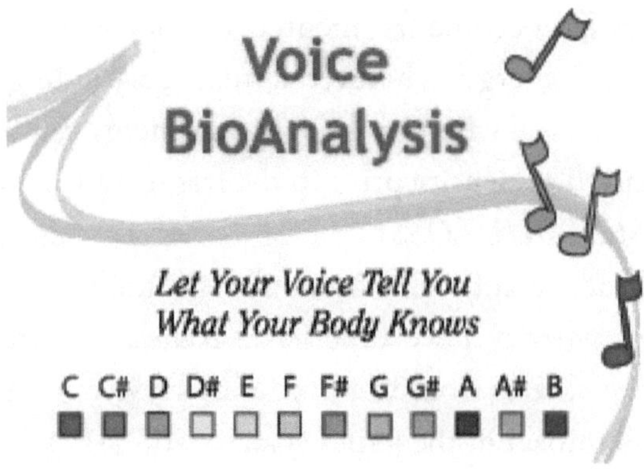

You can learn more about Voice Bioanalysis and hoe it can benefit you and your clients at my WebPage[1]

---

1. https://www.lanajthomas.com/voicebio.html

As you may already know, the practice of shamanism often includes psychically entering a client's body to find the dark or depleted energy field. The darkened field (shadow) is then expunged energetically, and it is replaced by powerful clean energy that the organ requires to heal properly. That new energy would be the right frequency for that organ or system. It is at this point that the healer trusts their team or guides to provide the proper frequency unless your extensive studies have granted that you know which frequency to impart with your healing hands. Energy medicine is becoming more scientific in its application and with that our healing is given more credence and potential for physical healing than we have had before.

Most now agree that the cellular memory of the body is what is holding the unhealthy memory/field in the body. It can also be a weakened area of the spirit that has become fragmented and needs to be reintegrated with the lost soul energy...wherever it may be residing. This is the process of soul retrieval whereby the spiritual energy can be restored to its original strength or density prior to the fragment leaving.

WHAT CAUSES SOUL LOSS?

According to leading authority on soul loss Sandra Ingerman, "The basic premise is whenever we experience trauma, a part of our vital essence (spirit) separates from us in order to survive the experience by escaping the full impact of the pain." (Gaia Staff, 2017)

> "With graceful delivery of rarely discussed phenomena, *Soul Retrieval: Mending the Fragmented Self* combines shamanism[2] and psychology to explain the effects of trauma that cause parts of the soul to leave the body and the process by which the part(s) can be retrieved[3]."

The Ayahuasca experience will lead to the discovery of the barrier of the cellular energy that blocks the opportunity to experience life fully.

---

2. https://www.gaia.com/article/how-much-do-you-know-about-shamanism

3. https://www.gaia.com/video/healing-luminous-body

The discovery of the self/the ego and how it preserves its status leads one to finally see outside the self and the bitterness and anger we tend to hoard. When a person vomits after drinking the psychedelic brew the memory has been expunged and in the end the bitterness and anger loses its grip on the soul. It is liberating and bewildering at the same time, because the 'me' the 'I' now takes on so much less significance and the person has a mirror to see themselves honestly.

Research the link below before moving on.

<u>The brutal mirror What the psychedelic drug ayahuasca showed me about my life.</u>[4]

Following angel assisted introspection and release, thought becomes clearer and less jaded by emotion and old thought patterns that hinder healing. Healing is hindered in the respect that when person is stuck in old thought patterns, new thought patterns cannot take root and grow into enlightened healing enhancing thought. It is in the freedom to think of healing as the norm, health as possible, freedom from childish hurts and anger as attainable that one can begin to heal. Then, then my friend do they begin to realize the beauty of the truth of the wonder of being part of something so much larger than the self.

So, the soul sickened person becomes freed from the limitations that thought which is centered upon the self has created. They are now able to receive energy that vibrates at a density that grant them healing. The same process can be energetically versus chemically replicated. I have personally experienced it at the helping hands of my guides and angels. As they led me through the painless process, it was explained to a me as identifying the Shadows hidden deep within my body and shining light upon them. The light was truth. I had lied to myself for years about certain feelings I had stored. I hid them because they were useless to

---

4. https://dmttimes.com/world-news/2019/7/26/the-brutal-mirror-what-ayahuasca-showed-me-about-my-life

react to. My reaction to them was anger but the anger expressed never altered anything.

So, they were stored away in the darkness of my spiritual field. Some it seemed were in the area of my liver. Others in the pelvic area of my body. You see I knew where the angels were looking for the shadows because I could feel their energy moving about inside me and I also felt a part of the exploratory team because they talked me through it. Together we discovered where the energy was less than optimal and cleared it away energetically by shifting it out of my body. Then, as the light of new energy was instilled the truth settled in.

Again, they talked to me and explained what they had found. The revelation that the major emotional wound I had been licking and nurturing was not true was life changing. I had deluded myself for many years and when I accepted what had really caused me pain in life and I tearfully let it go I was able to alter the course my life would take. I had held on to the version of what happened years back based on my perceptions as a child. Instead, it was merely 'what was' as a facet in the dynamics of human frailties will exhibit in life. The truth as revealed with the shift in energy allowed me to see the events of my childhood through the eyes of an adult.

What is so significant in this matter is that I was not looking for that truth at all. It was what was revealed to me. In this instance, it is like the Ayahuasca experience. The person when taking the herbal brew sets an intention by asking a question of the spiritual realm such as "What have I become?" My intent, in conjunction with the intent of my healing circle was to rid myself of roadblocks to my growth and my guides knew what was most relevant to me. The act of finding the Shadow can be conducted in several ways but the most efficient and safe is to have the angel assisting in your healing enter the person and find the shadows.

In this manner, the person's right to privacy is not violated and the healing is not interrupted at length with a counseling session which should be left to professionals. Spiritual healing is less traumatic than recounting one's youth or past with the purpose of purging the pain. Instantaneous purging during the Shadow finding event can often result in tears, sighs or coughs and even twitching as the Shadow is released. During the Ayahuasca ceremony the person normally purges by vomiting and usually feels a release of what was discovered about themselves that has been a barrier to growth.

What we think will define us and bolster us up. What we think also has the power to destroy us spiritually, So, what types of phrases must become part of your inner vocabulary?

? In an unlimited universe, all healing is forthcoming.

? In a space filled with divine presence, all are then, divine, and well.

? When healing is sought it will be provided.

? When power is present no earthly energy can resist it

? None that dwell in the midst of the Divine can withhold healing energy when it is sought. The power will be granted.

? If one thinks he or she is healed, it will be done. Thought energy is divine energy, so think accordingly.

? Gratitude is subliminal healing energy; it subjugates doubt to irrelevance.

** A body and mind that wishes to be well can connect to the divine healing energy ever present in the spiritual mind which holds earthly limiting thoughts at bay and opens the mind to the miraculous**

Now, if you think on these phrases always, you can withstand any onslaught of illness and angst. Remember, mentalism and thought energy are your most powerful allies. While you dwell on these thoughts, allow them to become a part of your belief system. It is not that they have to be repeated with redundancy, it that the words have to absorbed into your being and become a part of your life. When they are part of your life, instilled consciously in your mind, then they will become that which you are, and you will become a divine healer. What is in your mind is what will flow from your mind. Thus, you will easily project healing energy just by thinking about doing it.

Wisdom dictates that you cannot project healing power if you doubt that you have it or do not believe that it exists within you. That is simply logical in respect to stimulating healing power. It must have a source that it originated from, and that source is your mind that serves as the connection to healers who deliver the healing power through your own field. If you can see the fields or patterns that are being transmitted, then all the better because you can cooperate with the flow by increasing or decreasing the field, pattern, and the speed with which it is flowing, but first you must believe you are indeed capable of transmitting undefeatable healing power.

Life is exhibited in your beliefs and if your beliefs are limiting versus limitless in their content, you will by the natural course of thought, limit your healing ability. You can change your power simply by changing your mind, even in an instant of troubling times and trials. (Angels call it an attitude adjustment) Practice changing your mind if you want to change your life. If you are one who never changes their mind, then you are like stagnant water that is not hospitable to your body or your life.

Stagnant water lacks oxygen and renewal, and stagnation brings death. In those who are able to change their mind (thoughts) renewal is abundant and fresh life-giving energy flows freely. To elaborate on such a powerful message, Emerson said, "If I have lost my confidence in myself, I have the universe against me." Contrarily, if you have full confidence in your healing ability and your power, the universe will stand strong with you against any challenge. This message translates well to daily challenges posed upon us by living in this dimension.

If we allow ourselves to feel defeated, then naturally, we will be just that. Today's Shaman knows that living in the past, with its teachings and practices, may limit one's ability to tap into the powerful new energy offered to us today. Today's Shaman perceives that change and growth are an integral part of life because change is constant. Change is required by all who wish to reach the pinnacle of healing power. Acceptance of change ensures that you will be open to any new healing experience that may be required with each new client, because there is no set pattern of energy healing. The literal healing energy pattern may, of necessity, be different for every client. Isn't that exciting?

It means that healing energy is limitless, not only its supply, but specificity as well. Please note and remember: The most vital change that has taken place regarding healing power is that with recent dimensional shifts it is much easier for angelic healers to connect with us. This translates to the fact that it is now easier for us to connect with them as well. If you doubt your ability to hear clearly, even if you do not doubt your ability to heal, you may cast doubt on what you are being instructed to do. Each healing event must be viewed as similar to a tutorial and a new learning experience. The healer's job is to comply with instructions with gratitude and willingness.

~Those most willing will do the most. -Lana J. Thomas

Not only are we the conduit of the energy that flows to our clients, but we are also the conductors of it. In learning how to increase the flow of energy pulsing through your body you can magnify its result. People have differing methods of building the energy that courses through them. Some will clap their hands together then rub then vigorously together until they feel the energy tingling in their fingertips. Others simply focus thoughts of increased energy into their hands until the heat produced increases noticeably. No one way is right or wrong and is distinct to each healer.

One method Raphael recently taught me was that of lying or sitting comfortably and then imagining a ball of light in my uplifted palms. The ball I imagined in each hand was light blue in color and was spinning round afloat above my palms. Further instructions prompted me to begin to squeeze the ball like one would a rubber stress ball. I never really closed my hand all the way, I instead visualized compressing the ball and rolling it around in my hand. The more I squeezed, the more tension I felt. It was as if I could not have closed my hand if I wanted to. I knew when I had substantial energy compressed and the energy was for my own benefit or for that of another.

It was a training session, so I used the energy for myself by pushing it into my solar plexus and inhaling deeply. Then, I dispersed the energy throughout my body with intentional thought. It was so invigorating, and my mind felt so much sharper too. This exercise can be duplicated by any healer before a healing session and the resulting high vibration energy then used for the healing. A multitude of procedures are available, but this particular method is tangible because you can feel the energy grow denser and you can create more power when it is needed. Denser energy is the same as areas in dimensions that surround us thus you know you have a greater chance of raising the vibrational energy of your ill and weakened client when the energy is concentrated into a small space like the ball.

Your Thoughts Can Change the Mind of Another

About fifteen years ago, after a long battle with cancer, a dear friend of mine passed away. After her funeral she visited me very briefly. She quickly, without explanation, stated, "You could have healed me if you had learned how to control my mind!" As quickly as she came, she left. I stood my mouth open in readiness to ask her questions. I was stupefied! She had felt compelled to come and let me know that she had learned something of great value to me in the short time she had been gone.

But because she offered no explanation and neither did anyone I queried; I knew it was information that would be clarified at the appropriate time. Since Raphael has asked me to write this book, he has offered the explanation via the understanding of *mentalism.* As odd as the statement may seem, it has credibility and just how much is left to us to determine by learning how to change how another thinks.

Some may shy away from what could be called thought control but consider this well-known fact: 80% of all illnesses are caused by the mind...Thus, mentalism plays a vital role in healing.

The mental state of your client will determine the result you achieve together. It is obvious that if the mind can cause illness, it can also be reprogrammed to heal the body by thinking in a different way. You see, people who fear becoming ill may cause their body to contract the very illness they are afraid of. Fear creates a self-fulfilling prophecy. If one stops being afraid, they can alter how their body responds to attacks from invasive bacteria, inflammation, and a multitude of disease states. If you hope to heal a client, you must have within your grasp, the ability to change how they think so healing power can instill a new line of thinking in the client. It is relative to thought control, but simply positive and non-invasive in nature.

You might think of it as energetic hypnosis because it creates an altered state of awareness by suggesting to the mind that it can perceive things differently. If you are correcting the energy patterns of a client, by a natural course of inevitability, they will begin to think differently because the energy flowing through them will also alter how their neurons function. Even their synapses will fire with a renewed spark and their hormones will respond in kind. Hormones regulate the body, its heat, its immune response, its metabolism, and its energy. So, energy must first focus on the thought energy of the client and change is initiated by asking your healing circle to adjust thought patterns and energy levels in their brain. Trust is an imperative at this juncture in the healing process of angel assisted healing.

The focus of the physical body and its state of illness is relegated to less importance than the vibration of the spirit of the client. When the healer and the client trust completely a healing circle will determine what is right for the person at that moment and the truth that is proffered by the shift in consciousness and the following shift in perception will result in the client having less desire to be ill. A person who is ill will never acknowledge that the illness serves a purpose because that seems illogical, and it minimizes illness to a blaming the sick person for being ill. This is not what the angels want us to understand.

Rather, it is that a weakly spirited person will because their spiritual energy is weak become ill by the very nature of being weak and vulnerable. Beyond that, healing angels would have us understand that our perception of mind body spirit should be flipped to spirit mind body. The spirit must be primary, and it must be of a high and sustained vibration or the spirit/consciousness of that person will opt to leave in order that it may find the connection with the divine once again. If it must leave the body to do so...it will. For a spirit to leave a body is nothing more than a move for the spirit because it is eternal as energy and cannot die.

It can be explained as the spirit cannot maintain the body if it is weak and malnourished as spirit. Therefore, to be a healer means the shaman's goal is to deliver spiritual power through healing energy, so the spirit is strong and vibrant. A vibrant spirit has the desire to live and recovery is then possible. Illness is not something that happens to the person, quite the contrary. Illness just is a part of our lives just like storms and accidents are. They may be perceived as something very negative if one believes them to be. However, the many facets of reality in this dimension may not all be what we might perceive as a blessing but nonetheless it is our present reality. Illness, pain, suffering of many sorts are just part of life.

As such, knowing that it is not done to us but instead for us removes the fear that we are being judged or punished. The shift in perceptions come when the angels realign thought to coincide with truth and logic. When the thought vibration is heightened to a density that vibrates with the enlightenment the illness is no needed. It is no longer needed by the person who is weak emotionally psychologically and spiritually because they begin to experience self-empowerment and no longer feel compelled to rely upon others attention.

The illness is no longer needed as a tool by their spirit to gain their attention, create fear of death and make the person seek life. The crux of the matter is this, according to the Archangel Raphael, a healer cannot alter what another believes, nor should they because each person is where they are for a reason which will be revealed to them in time if they seek answers, but by allowing energy to shift the vibration of their field they are more likely to seek answers.

When they question, they will get answers. The answers will push them toward enlightenment and enlightenment will grant that they become part of the evolution of consciousness. The more they are a part of the shifts taking place the more enlightened they will become. It is cyclical. It is powerful. What would normally take years of therapy to work through can be revealed and expunged in a matter of minutes. The purging of Shadows makes way for illumination and illumination makes way enlightenment. In this manner, the angels see struggle and suffering as a way. The enlightened person finds that way, and thus can move forward to find the Way. The reason that the angels require that we as healers not attempt to change what another believes is because the person who has been cleansed of shadows will find the Way but only by finding their own way.

We must not interfere with the enlightenment process by inflicting the person further with what they should believe because we do not know. That is right! We do not have those answers! The client's guides know what they should believe. The angels know what the client should believe so it is reasonable to allow them to hunt for shadows that lurk in their energy field. Furthermore, the angels know just how much truth the person can bear the weight of at one time. The weight they release in the purge will lighten them immensely however, change will ensue and change rarely comes easy. So, healing angels know just the right dosage that will awaken the person to just what new truth they are to pursue on their path to purpose.

Getting specific: If you ask the clients personal guides to assist, they are the experts in this matter because they know the client better than they know themselves. Remember you want specialists on board and their guides have known them all their lives, have heard every thought, and know of memories that hold them back. Healing memories first, is a good line of defense and will result in better healing results. If your client is present, in the now, they are more capable of accepting the healing energy without interference from negative or troubling thoughts. Try this experiment to reaffirm how thought energy works.

Pay very close attention to how your day goes when you are feeling down or experiencing low energy. Your perception of your world or immediate environment, such as your job and performance, will directly reflect what you experience. It is integral to note that how you perceive your environment can be totally false. Everybody around you can be fine, happy, and at peak performance but you will perceive it as the opposite because that is where your mind and thoughts have taken you. If you can alter how you see the day, the world, your view of your performance, then you can change your world...as you see it. It is a shift in consciousness and ultimately perception which by its natural course, becomes your new reality.

~It may come as a severe shock if you haven't given much thought to this subject before, but our precious, cast-in-stone, objective beliefs are often totally in contrast to any reality. Or, more accurately, they are our perception of reality, rather than reality itself. ~Robert White

To experience mentalism on a physical level: Sit in a quiet room and begin mentally talking to your heart. Tell it to calm itself and beat more slowly. Send that thought projected energy to your heart and you will literally feel your heartbeat begin to slow and strengthen. Talk to your immune system and encourage it to persist in attacking viruses and disease. The result works better than Tamiflu™ if you have contracted a virus because your mind can heal your body when you understand the way it heals itself and work in conjunction with it.

This process is frequently used in hospitals and is called Biofeedback. The device one is attached to measures the results and feeds the information back to the patient who is taught to respond to the information by trying harder to control their body's responses or relax and instill the result. It is very successful for people with high or low blood pressure. It is energy medicine. It can be done without the device too. So, it is important to educate your clients about how they think about their illness and have them think about their health instead. Fear of illness must be rejected as unnatural and foolhardy.

Fear indicates a lack of knowledge of how the body is beautifully designed to maintain a healthy state. Furthermore, fear is negatively charged energy and it does nothing to promote healing, in fact, it attracts negative energy into the body's field simply because like attracts like. Have you ever noticed that some people love to talk about their illnesses?

Some wear illness like a badge of notoriety. Once they start telling you about how sick they are, it is next to impossible to get them to stop. This happens because as they tell you about it, they are robbing you of your life-giving energy in order to feed their depleted energy field. All too often, we feel we must be empathetic and listen for hours, and yet, while they have stolen your energy, it will sadly be used to feed the illness, not their health, because that is what they are thinking about and thus the energy they expend will bolster the disease. One may even make a person sicker by letting them talk about how sick they are.

Care must be taken to talk of how healing results and not how illness destroys.

Do not give your precious energy to those unfortunate people. If you do, they will keep coming back for more until you become too weak to supply them. Then they will find another victim to suck the life out of.

Stop the momentum before it begins by giving them a loving (healing) hug and try asking, "So, what positive things are you doing to heal yourself?" Take control of the conversation, in other words, and then share your amazing knowledge with them and you will both be lifted to a higher energy pattern. Sadly, people who love being ill cannot heal!

Too often, people embrace illness to get attention because they are lonely or have simply never learned how to attract positive attention. If you have clients such as this, your work must begin by changing their mind and its energetic patterns and, of course, how they view illness. Illness will never be their friend and should always be rejected as a companion. Compare their obsession with their illness with this scenario:

They are hiking in the mountains; the air is clean and fresh. They are filled with peace and possibilities of a fine experience. Suddenly, ahead of them on the path appears a huge mountain lion. Terrified, they run, not away from the lion, but directly toward the cat. They kneel and fully embrace the predator...And you know how that story inevitably ends because the cat is hungry. If one embraces a disease, coddles it and loves it because they get attention from it, the disease will, because it is predatory nature, eventually eat them. The process is dangerous in either situation.

How one perceives illness plays an integral role in recovery! Over the years, much research has been done on perception and the results have indicated that limited perceptions of the world one inhabits is based solely upon what they know and understand about their world, i.e., what they have experienced. If a client has never experienced vibrant health and a happy attitude, then it will be very difficult for that person to think in a way that reflects vibrancy and health.

Today's Shaman understands that care must be taken to correct how the client thinks by granting the energy of love...the energy that supersedes all others. Thus, when you hug a client, let the loving energy you are connected with flow into them through you. Let your efforts to correct negative energy fields within them be conducted with a loving energy you have borrowed from the universe. It is this loving energy that the Archangels want us to take advantage of because it will change the world around us. Imagine a world without judgement and hatred. Imagine a world where we rise, figuratively and literally, into a higher dimension of thought and clarity. We can do this for mankind one step at a time by shifting the consciousness of humans who desire to dwell in a higher dimension of belief and perception of the loving energy of etheric beings as integral to creating change that alters our future.

We can help the angels alter our perceptions by agreeing to connect with them and let them heal us. Between you and me-the angelic realm is ready to open wide the doors of healing and let new more powerful healing flow forth. Today's Shaman sees the bigger picture and the need for all of us to alter our perceptions of how healing begins in the mind...

> *Mankind must know: "They themselves are makers of themselves" by virtue of the thoughts which they choose and encourage; that mind is the master weaver, both of the inner garment of character and the outer garment of circumstance, and that, as they may have hitherto woven in ignorance and pain they may now weave in enlightenment and happiness. ~As a Man Thinketh-James Allen*

You may feel a bit overwhelmed with the concept, however those who will create the shifts through us are fully equipped to bring about change. The degree of speed with which it happens depends upon how much we trust them to work through us. A major part of healing consists of correcting the psychological disparity first and bringing the mind to a place of health. If a person thinks about how sick they are, they are directing thought energy to the illness and essentially feeding it. Health Psychologists strive to alter the way a person thinks about illness by educating them in how their body is impeccably designed to heal. They understand how psychological, behavioral, and cultural factors contribute to physical health and illness.

Their research shows that health is a trickle-down process, in that one's brain controls the entire body. Like a computer, the brain sends out signals to every cell and organ and tells them what to do. A mind that dwells on illness perpetuates disease and a depleted brain cannot provide the correct signals to the body. For example, depression leads to a low energy flow to the body and its systems. A brain exhausted by stress lacks the energy to sustain the body and the signals the brain sends can be inadequate to manage the delicate balance of a healthy state. Both anxiety and stress are a part of life today, and yet if one can alter the way they respond to stress and draw upon healing energy that restore their mental state they stand a much greater chance of recovery. By helping people to change the way they perceive their world, a healer can assist their client at a core level. Does a healer have to be a health psychologist? No, of course not, but they do have to understand that the brain is the control center and use energy healing to alter the brain waves. It is possible to lift the depressive energy and replace it with a feeling of peace and love. It is up to the client to sustain the change by altering the way they think about being sick. They must understand this, even if you have to blunt by stating that fact, not only by conveying that message boldly, but also in your actions as a healer.

You must help them understand that it is an imperative that they love their body through the healing process, and they do that by altering how they perceive what energy is capable of providing for them. Once you have enabled them to experience the healing energy and how it flows through their body their perception of healing and attitude toward healing and healthy thoughts will take root. I always warned my family that when they got sick, if they lay down and embrace the disease, it will worsen.

The resiliency of healing energy flows when one denies the strength of the disease as the stronger force. Healing comes from thinking, "I am the master of my body and its ability to heal. Love is greater than disease and I will rise above this. I will stand up and fight, not lie down and wallow in the mire of illness." (Note: There are always exceptions to every rule and, of course, some illnesses require rest and restoration. The admonishment to stand and fight is figurative as well as literal in this sense.)

"You have the power to heal yourself, and you need to know that. We think so often that we are helpless, but we are not. We always have the power of our minds. Claim and consciously use your power." Louise Hay
Help your clients see a more positive view of health and how significant it is that they think healthy thoughts. It used to be considered confrontational to tell someone that their illness was all in their head (imagined), but the imagination is a powerful source of creation, as we are learning, and imagined illness becomes real when one directs energy toward it. A person's thoughts can dictate whether their body's canvass is painted with vibrant colors of health or dark muted colors of disease.

'The mind, once stretched by a new idea, never returns to its original dimensions.' ~Oliver Wendell Holmes-
Healing begins with you! What pieces come together for you in the time it takes you to read this book will determine what parts of your personal puzzle you begin to put in place. For some it will be the

idea of living a life without emotions ruling their life. To be stable and balanced emotionally is quite contrary to nearly every genre of life today. Everything is based how much drama is generated by acts, relationships, communities, and experiences that can be shared on social media. In a "see me" culture of selfies and self-absorption we are deluged with the drama and excitement of others once private lives.

Reactions and emotions run high over the slightest thing and if we cannot feel strong emotions, we can be led to believe we are not truly living. Becoming stable emotionally and not being ruled by emotions will entail great maturity and self-restraint. If you consider that being without fluctuating emotions throughout the day could lead to our being more like ascended masters that we wish to model, then learning the art of self-control is an important part of our lives as healers. To keep the self in balance requires self-exploration and self-examination in instances where life does not seem balanced and negative energy creeps in around us.

A pause to reflect on what is different about the way things are going on any given day, especially if the day seems negatively charged, is necessary to narrow down what adjustments in thoughts are required to bring the energy field in and around you back into synchronization with energies that feel comfortable and healthy emotionally and psychologically. To be more succinct, to keep one's energy vibrating at a high level, one must be on guard and monitor the mood of the day and act accordingly to circumvent the negative unhealthy energies from creeping in. And it is this private endeavor is what will keep you strong energetically.

Contrary to this type of introspection is the mode of looking outside the self and projecting blame upon another. Thoughts like "I was fine until my boss criticized my performance. She made me feel inadequate and sad. Now my day has gone south, and I feel a bit angry." Blaming others for one's reactions to daily life events is useless to positively alter anything. Understanding that she or he is probably doing their job of managing others and respect for their need to please their own boss can alleviate the negative energy. Empathy and love for that manager will bring balance back into your mind and emotions will subside with the right type of thoughts being transmitted to your body and field.

To make the concepts of universal love and energy part of your being, you must live the precepts in your daily life. You cannot separate your private life from your life and practice as a healer. In order to be part of the circle that is Today's Shaman you must project power over the details of life that will cause you to struggle. Power comes from thought and right thinking. Power comes from power, so you must maintain the power to be powerful. Otherwise, you must constantly go back through the processes whereby you attained it in the first place. Trust me, it is easier to stay on task and maintain your power than it is to suffer the loss of it.

Oh my god, that place is a lonely forsaken place because now you truly know the difference and you will feel the loss of power on a much greater level. You will grieve the loss just like when you lose a loved one. I hope you never find yourself there. Sorrow, deep sorrow, can take you to a dark place that is hard to find your way out of. It is separation from the divine source and a sick spirit will cause your mind to suffer until you find your way back. Life gets in the way sometimes; we feel alone, and we also get homesick often. We feel the pull of the other side. We live in two worlds. Theirs and ours and ours does not always fit the way things flow in theirs. We are as the scripture states, "In this world but not of it." We are different. We are different in a marvelously intrinsic manner that wells from the soul within us.

It does cause us the pain of loneliness at times but that type of loneliness is a trifle compared the relinquishment of our power. Being powerless also entails a total lack of freedom. A lack of freedom causes us to fear, and fear destroys our faith. It is a viscous cycle that I think we all encounter at dark-times in our lives. Thankfully, we have spirit guides who bolster us up and push us on toward our goals. Fortunately, each struggle with soul sickness results in a an even greater impetus to move on, take another step, reach out for help, and let the healing begin yet again.

This is growth. This mystery is part of being human. Thankfully, with each hurdle we jump and find ourselves again on the other side brings us closer to divinity and lessens the chance that we will ever have to sink into that mire ever again. You see, we can come to understand that we can be different, even more different than other people, because we are less like humans and more like the divine nature we are instilled with from birth. We just lost our way for a bit while we were looking for ourselves.

If we are enlightened and our minds have been trained to think on a higher level, we can circumvent the reactions to living that got us stuck in the first place. I have been clinging to the concept that Raphael put forth of living with purpose and not reacting emotionally to anything that is happening around me. I find it so liberating. It is hard to describe in words. Initially I was baffled by his message of needing those who were emotionless...then as he clarified that love is an energy and we are energy then it became clear that I wanted to be more loving. Honestly, my goal for years has been to finally live at a vibration so far above the low density of this life that I will never have to return to earth as I have known in it this life.

I want to be a master of my destiny. I want to be a master of the 7th density like those who have graciously come to teach me about who I am and could be. This goal is not grandiose. Let's think of it as possible, attainable, and ever so necessary if we want to live what has been our purpose all along. The higher they enable us to raise our vibration and power, the more we will understand that we are able to rise above the darkness of injustice, hate, inequality, and fury that still needs healing in this dimension. The more we rise about it all, the more we understand why they want us to change. Try not give in to doubt that we can ever have an impact on the world. It only takes a spark to ignite a fire.

Now after Raphael came and asked me to write this book, the more I think about what he has led me to research, study and contemplate, the more I understand that the fire he wants to start with a new healing energy as the key to our future. It all seems sensible and logical. We must be different to make a difference. If we are not different, then we are the same. We should want to rise above the mire and the muck and want to be forever unstuck. It is divine that we want to be free and most of all...want to be happy. That is all they have ever wanted for us.

For instance, no matter who I have been visited by or what the details were that were conveyed, the crux of the visit was always the always the same. They would ask, "Lana, where is your joy?" Then I could never answer other than to say, "I wish I knew!" As the years have passed and I have climbed many hurdles in search of myself, I go deeper as I go higher. I go deeper into myself and honestly look at my self-made struggles. The same is true of every seeker. Emotional intelligence has taught us to look inward not outward. Maturity has granted that we understand and are capable of being happy and content in just being. We do not have to emote, do not have to react, because we know even though any given situation that seems difficult..."*is what it is*" yet we *must also remind ourselves, 'but it is not what it could be.*"

To say helplessly," Oh well, it is what is" is not sufficient onto the task of wanting and creating change. To learn to raise your vibration is to realize such will raise your level of conscious thought to becoming aware that there is a deeper purpose to rising above a situation. It can be literal. One can energetically rise above. And there in that peaceful space, be happy. When we have risen above and look back onto the situation, we become conscious that change is possible, and change will alter what is- *no matter what it is*. And change begins with each one of us. We are the spark.

It is with a bit of trepidation that I share that on a more seemingly selfish note, I always remind myself that my goal, my ultimate goal is to find my highest self. I owe that to me. I have worked hard to understand all the messages of hope when I felt hopeless. I have opened my mind to seemingly senseless information I was determined to make sense of knowing it was only my limitations as a human that prevented me from understanding universal concepts. I know that wisdom is power. I know that learning is the path to wisdom.

I trust logic and I trust my guides and all those who come to reason with me. I know that truth is like an elusive lover and more I pursue it the more it will seduce me and beckon me forth for even deeper truths...my truths in this lifetime that are higher truths I will keep in the next. All the messages that have been offered were meant to be shared with others. It is not about me. It never was. It is about the oneness of consciousness and sharing the steps all can take. Wisdom is free and available to any who seek to be enlightened and uplifted to higher thought and intellect.

(Secret~ The Archangels willingly increase our intellect if we allow them access to our brain! Just get quiet and ask them to come.)

The Archangels and your Guides wish for us to learn and become all we capable of and if you will grant them permission to change your life they will steadfastly do so.

I offer you this knowledge in an eCourse on Udemy entitled Beginners Universal Feng Shui[5]. It is a course in learning to trust the angels with total access to your home and family. In doing so, your life and degree of happiness and joy will become your lifestyle.

***Trust me it is less about Feng Shui than it is about changing your life...see a difference in 9 days and dramatic shift in 9 months just by allowing them into your space and using the special symbols they had me design for you**.*

Inspirational Quotes to Consider:

---

5. *https://www.udemy.com/course/beginners-universal-feng-shui/*

"There is an alchemy in sorrow. It can be transmuted into wisdom, which, if it does not bring joy, can yet bring happiness."
—*Pearl Buck*

"Be patient with yourself. Self-growth is tender; it's holy ground. There's no greater investment." —*Stephen Covey*
"When we seek for connection, we restore the world to wholeness. Our seemingly separate lives become meaningful as we discover how truly necessary we are to each other."
—*Margaret Wheatley*

Chapter Six: Your Journey is Priority

I sometimes think that I am selfish when making my growth my priority in all ways. It has to be first and foremost on my mind at all times or the muck of life's relationships and interactions will pull me back down. The beauty of the message as it unfolds is that via the power of mentalism, healers can make a difference. If by thinking differently and deliberately projecting that thought into the field of consciousness, then those (maybe many people) in harmony with it will receive that vibration and the exponential effects of them sending it on can be staggering. This is not a new concept, now I know that if we project that thought with powerful intent and use our minds as an antenna that we can catapult the message of powerful vibrational energy, the new energy we are being granted now, and greatly increase the resulting effect on humanity.

This energy has been building for a definite purpose and design. It is not just that we can heal one body or dozens of bodies. We can heal the crippling diseased energy that is pervading our world. As I understand it, the more the vibration of the planet rises, the more unsettled the minds and bodies of humanity become. Especially of those who have no concept of what is going on. Billions of people have no connection to the higher vibrations and nonetheless are directly affected by them. If they cannot accept the changes for the better that are coming, they can literally be driven mad by them. Every living soul has a place in the universe. That is why they are so intent on finding meaning in money or notoriety. Sadly, we have been taught to believe that success is materialistic.

Every person knows that they are indeed entitled to be part of a much larger picture of accomplishment and success in life. Because the entitlement is very real it spurs them on, but so regrettably in the wrong direction. When success is not forthcoming, the new energy still pushes them on and on. It does so just by its nature of being an agent of change. Madness settles in the form of greed and want for more of anything that might make them feel they are finally getting their fair share. This madness leads to the list of depraved behaviors which crowds our morning news with dreadful stories of how another has fallen and has taken victims with them. Insanity is defined as not knowing the difference between right and wrong. Insane people believe they are right and everyone else is wrong.

Unfortunate souls are caught up in the madness and unless they are brought to truth of the shifts in consciousness and how the world must change and is changing, they will sink even deeper to an even lower dimension of thought. We are living in the 3rd dimension by definition, and they will be plunged back into the 2nd and even the 1st dimension. What dwells there is scary as hell. Regrettably we must deal with them in the meantime and suffer the attacks, the murders, the rapes, sexual slavery, and heinousness of all the egregious things they do. We feel helpless to stop the suffering and insanity. Furthermore, the planet is feeling the powerful shifts and waves of energy that are flowing through here. It is causing upheaval of the most frightening kinds. Hurricanes, tsunamis, earthquakes, and global threats of destruction are with us each day now. Many will die as a result. Though this information is unsettling it explains a lot!

In attempts to understand what is coming in the future by asking of guides and Archangels if they are at liberty to share with us what the result will be when the energy is stabilized. I immediately get a check that the energy will not stabilize because that would mean it had become stagnant. But the timing of the changes is integral to our cooperative spirit and what we perceive now and in the future. We can be of the past and adhere to old ways and be just fine for a very long time or we can abandon what we have been taught to believe and look to the evidence of a new day and a new world.

We can hear the whispers on the winds of change, and we can see the waves of newness that transforms so many from what was to what is to be. The idea that we are going to find ourselves in despair and destruction is not what we want to adhere to. Even thought for thousands of years we have been anticipating and fearing the destruction of darkness and the ascension into light.

We may be most pleasantly surprised by the movement of thought to alter what has held so many in darkness and disillusionment. We can feel the revelation of a new day and not the promise of judgment and destruction of the darker side for the reprisal of light. Let me explain...the way we have been taught to believe is that everywhere are two forms of being, i.e., light and dark. One good and one bad.

What if there were a significant coalition of those who would be considered neutral or somewhat grey? How would neutrality affect the politics of the day and how would complacency affect the overabundance of drama in the world? Would a very vast gathering of neutral people who did not subscribe to any one view specifically find themselves living outside the constructs of the world's view of might makes right?

If so, how would that affect the lives of billions who see only one way as the right way? If people stopped competing and offered a hand to others that may be trying to find some equality in the world, would the lack of competition affect the outcome of those who push to be first at the risk of shoving others back down the ladder? It would have a positive effect on those who are trying to find fairness as a way of life and yet, for people to believe that they can give up competing and striving to best everyone else is to ask the impossible of most. Try to imagine a universe wherein everyone is equal in stature and respect. It takes some doing does it not because everything we have built our lives upon is based upon getting ahead, putting down, winning by making others lose, and taking more than our share.

Regrettably, our governments typify greed and want for power. It is all we know. It is all we have ever known! And yet, is it possible that alternatives exist? Yes, of course it is possible! Is it probable that without intervention we would ever find a plausible workable alternative? No! Thus, in order that we may stay abreast of the changes that are coming in the rest of our universe we are witnessing divine intervention from beings that have tested and verified that other ways of existence are reasonable, plausible, and necessary to the path of the evolution of species that inhabit this universe. We believed for centuries that our existence was the center of God's universe and He was committed solely to our care. We have learned that nothing could be further from the truth and that we have come to terms with our place as a speck in the universes.

Instead of God healing us and preparing our way in love...He would rather that we learn to heal ourselves and take responsibility for reparations of our errors and plans to circumvent that our history keeps repeating itself. A strong psychological and spiritual premise is the theory of whom is most powerful or self-empowered...the one who subscribes to the idea of an internal locus of control or the one who believes everything is out of his or her control and fate and God are at the wheel at every turn.

In 1954, psychologist Julian Rotter suggested that our behavior was controlled by rewards and punishments and that it was these consequences for our actions that determined our beliefs about the underlying causes of these actions. Our beliefs about what causes our actions then influence our behaviors and attitudes. Individuals with an external locus of control believe they have little influence over the events of the world. Those who rely too heavily upon the spirit world of God for their every need and success will indeed have little influence over anything and they do not feel the need for it. They may say, "It is what it is." With a note of resignation in their voices, they resolve to deny responsibility for circumstances and the need to create change where necessary. Few are those who perceive the condition of life today as acceptable, just, and good. They are those who point fingers of blame and rarely look inward.

We have too many glaring problems that are faced by the multitudes to pretend that all is right with the world. We have made a mess of things and although we have not intentionally created situations and circumstances which are deleterious in nature, we have indeed created problems by neglect if not intent. We appoint officials to represent us and to govern in a way that should have been forward looking enough to prevent the problems we face and now we project the blame upon them and demand they create magic and repair the damage that has been done to our societies, planet, culture, and people. The stance we have taken is much more comfortable than that of looking inward to see what we can do ourselves. We only feel powerless if we want to feel powerless in order that we not have to act in whatever manner presents itself that can make a difference.

"We need to accept that we won't always make the right decisions, that we'll screw up royally sometimes—understanding that failure is not the opposite of success; it's part of success." —Arianna Huffington

There is a very line between expressing concern for the needs we have to change our world and just being a negative nuisance that brings others down. I do not subscribe to fatalistic thinking because I do not want to attract that kind of energy to myself or my family. But, let me say this, it is touted that some elusive sect or group truly understands the power of mentalism in its ability to create. The power it holds is not limited to good. Thus, by creating fear on a global scale and projecting lies through the internet and the media, people become manipulated into creating catastrophes and bring about our own destruction by the way we think. Our fear is that powerful.

Some declare population control is afoot as the fewer of us there are the more that is there for the greedy. Ironically, I have been told that it is that very group who will not be allowed to rise to a higher vibration and they will also sink to the 1st dimension to be tortured and ruled by a subhuman class of beings. It is the Law of Recompense at work. Karma or recompense will deal with those who had attained the highest degree of affluence and information and kept it all to themselves instead of doing something to benefit mankind.

My source of information was Quetzalcoatl, the Mayan messiah. He came to me about a decade ago and asked if he could work with me for a while. Not having the slightest idea who he was at the time, via research I found all I could about him and the Mayan way of life. It was a life of egalitarianism. Everyone contributed, and everyone benefited equally. It was the most prolific societies the earth has ever known.

Anyway, he taught me about what it really meant to be on earth, why we are all here and that our one goal in life was to learn how to be 'good' enough to not ever have to come back here. He explained that he felt deeply for my plight in being here and that in his experience it was most dreadful. He despised the way every thought and every deed had to be weighed and measured as to whether it was right or wrong. Our systems are established upon judgement. Especially when God's image is distorted to that of judge.

He did not appreciate the nature of judgementalism that accompanies existence here. He explained that we are here to learn how to live elsewhere or literally on a higher plane of existence. We for whatever personal reasons or history have been deemed unfit to live with those who are at a higher vibration. We have the purpose of learning how to be different or better. We have grown so much in a decade that we understand this is like a place for juvenile delinquents who are babies in the understanding of the greater universal truths. He said, "You are not hopeless, but you are a people without hope." That has always stuck with me because sometimes hope is all we can cling to when times get rough. I never felt that I was without hope because my faith to sustains me. But what of those who have none or those who had it and lost it and are now in that horrible dead zone of grief and sorrow.

The soul sickness of this planet is taking a huge toll. We are caught here for a time until the shifting is complete if we live that long. And, who truly knows how long that will take? So, the crux of the matter is, while we sort this all out and learn all we must learn to be 'good' enough, we cannot be idle in the interim. What this book is focused on is how we as Today's Shamans, can have an influence on the impact of the shift. We can heal people by raising their vibrations. We can affect the lives of others by learning to love unconditionally and at the same time affect the planet in a positive way using thought wave energy. If shamanism is the oldest form of spirituality that has not succumbed to traditional or conventional thought and religiosity then it makes sense that operating outside the restrictions of religion offers the higher likelihood that we can affect change. If you are reading this book you came to be an earth angel in whatever form you find yourself.

Shamans are, after all, those who work in a significantly different level of communication with the universe that is not limited to religion and ancient texts, which in turn, does not limit what they are willing to explore. Ours is a knowing based upon personal experiences and often contrary information that we garner from our spiritual exercises and journeys. Religion tends to restrict the freedom of explorers.

Furthermore, many religions fear explorers learning greater truths than the church accepts as historically correct based upon which ever text is adhered to, the Bible or Koran for example. It makes sense that if one learns truths outside the dogma of a sect then that same one is likely to leave that sect and strike out on their own. Remember the elusive group that is using lies to create a negative outcome? They are hidden, obscure and though many theories exist...we cannot be sure what to believe.

Because confusion is an effective tool used by them. Is it some globalized group of powerful elites who hold the mass of world's wealth in their greedy hands? Is it some universal group of galactic proportions manipulating the outcome or are they too just a pawn of the intergalactic elites here and who hope to inhabit the planet when millions are wiped out? Is it all the above? Conspiracy theories will continue to confound and confuse us, so we may never know. But those of infinite knowledge know so they will deal with it when the time is right. What is relevant is that we understand that a group need not be seen to be powerful. What we do in cooperation with the Archangels can have a profound impact. We can do it from the security of our own homes.

Quetzalcoatl left me with a quote that I hold dear. ~He said, "It is not about how visible you are, but about how effectively you can create visible change."

Every time I read that statement, I am humbled and yes, reminded that it is not fame and fortune that serves best. It is power! I desire the power to create positive change. That may sound a bit arrogant, however without power, I am powerless to effect change of any sort, even within myself, which is where it all starts. We fix the self and then become servants for the greater good. What I believe I have as a gift to offer is my desire to write and share what I am taught. Sharing may create a yawn in some folks, but it may create an explosion of awareness in another, and the other is the person being reached out to. I would never have learned what I have been taught by being afraid of seeking more...more of everything that the universe has to offer. My life was thus, forever changed.

The more I learn from guides, angels, and ET's, the more it is realized that in a life of obscurity and secretiveness, the more the power within solitude and searching for more elusive truths that beckon me forward. I do not have to be famous but do need to have access to creative power that grants that successfully reaching out to others to help expand the whole concept of enlightenment and thankfully, that power is being illuminated as mentalism. Mentalism is the same power used by forces that attempt to enslave us in fear and by using us subliminally, we may unwittingly manifest that which is not serving the highest good yet will serve those who wish to enslave us...like they already have.

Our fear becomes a self-fulfilling prophecy, in other words, because we keep putting fears out there in the etheric thought world and that is what we attract. Put simply, if enough of people fear the threat of war...the collective consciousness brings it forth to fruition because it must...that is just how it works. Contrarily, and thankfully, the more we collectively put forth loving energy and powerful thoughts of enlightenment and exponential enlightenment for all, the more we push back the negative fear filled energetic waves that are forming and becoming reality. It is not a war between good and evil, but it is a war. It is a war between It is What it is and What it Could Be. And everything could be sooooo much better!

Deep within all of us is the desire for happiness. We are all one, so some are not different than or better than others. We all have a purpose, which is to find our highest self. We may all take different paths to get there but getting there is tantamount to the eternal flow of the tides of growth and expansion of higher consciousness and spiritual awareness. If we pursue that train of thought and continue to help awareness expand, we may indeed all be happy someday. We can do just that when we stop being afraid and sitting in front of the TV, wringing our hands in despair while we view man's depravity and the injustices within our dimension. The tides right now are coming forth in tsunami like fashion and the powerful shifts are creating discomfort and fear in those who do not understand that the process is evolutionary and natural in its construct. Many theorize that the shifts cause the totally un-awakened to literally go mad.

That theory could answer many questions we have regarding the bizarre and brutal behavior of those who perform mass shootings such as those at Las Vegas and at public schools. It is true that if you do not shift into a higher density that you will be left behind in a much lower one and the disturbances there will cause further confusion and sinking even deeper. Many may interpret this as hell and that may be an apt description because it will certainly be a place of torment.

Pieces of the universal puzzle are coming together for some. For others, the picture is being crashed to the floor as beliefs and disbeliefs are being exposed to 'light thinking.' The thought of souls suffering because they never became exposed to a higher consciousness is sad. The forsaken will someday get another opportunity in an infinite time frame and yet, that is part of parcel of the idea of just giving in and acquiescing to fated destinies. It is possible that some people you know, and love could be among those who in stagnation and frustration, get stuck under a vast net of lies and misconceptions. As a forty-year student in communication with The Father, ET's, 7th density masters, and thousands of guides, I still do not profess to understand it all. But the pieces will continue to fall into place, and we will see through glass less dark, and clarity will be granted.

But remember, if we are blessed enough to be released from the 3rd density once and for all and dwell in the 5th density as many have strived for...we will be at the bottom of the learning curve there and begin my journey yet again, so we may entertain the thought of someday being in the 7th density or higher. That is then, and this is now...today we are learning about powerful energies that heal and understanding that we can make a difference even if it just a speck of light in the darkness that someone will use as a guide to their higher self and beyond. If healers like you will join in the pursuit of assisting others with their transmutation, we can impact so many more before the 'theys' (whoever they are) of the universes cause yet more destruction.

In Summation:

- We are on the cusp of dramatic shifts and the flow of energetic vibrations will only grow stronger as time passes.
- We either meet the flow with acceptance and reverence or we

succumb to the despair and desolation of madness.

- Today's shamans have the ability to create a magnetic flow of energy frequencies that can enable the process to be less violent.
- With the Laws of Mentalism as a guide to living an enlightened life we can rise above the fear of change and ride out the storms.
- We need tools at our disposal...energetic tools.
- We need power, and it comes from being those bold enough to embrace godly principles and stand fearlessly in the face of the enemy that seeks to destroy that which is profoundly important to the future of all that live in the light. Even if the enemy is not so clearly defined.
- We need to begin to ask for direction on a personal level and each one of us, in their own way, can then do whatever we can to assist the allied forces for good to bring about a new world.
- We will learn to manifest all that we need to remain strong, and we will be taught how to retain our strength as we seek guidance from those who desire, sincerely desire, to lead us onward to the path of righteousness.
- We can become a very powerful force that will fight the invisible with invisible energy and the war will usher in peace.

You should know by now if you have been selected to participate...have you?

Power Comes from Power

I have deliberately lived my life somewhat separated from the mainstream, preferring it like that because it is safer that way. I keep my life secret to keep it safe. I keep my plans secret to keep them safe. I am not paranoid nor afraid of being 'out there' anywhere. Yet, bringing myself to this point of enlightenment in this life has required great commitment and work and strife to suffer as little influence from darker forces as possible.

Dark forces are defined as anything that does not dwell in the light. Everyday life is filled with darker forces of another's drama, and it is easy to get sucked into the energy vampires who will steal your peace. When peace is gone, so is your power. Many are the struggling souls who are lost in the trials and tribulations of living and surviving. Those who know they are dying will unintentionally seek attention from anyone who will listen to their story. Beware! They seek to steal your power! Gossiping with people about others will create a Karmic backlash and even though we know that it is easy to get caught up in it. What is the news on TV, but gossip? What is good about hearing of another's suffering or mistakes if hearing of it does nothing to heal the harm and, in fact, adds to the destruction. Each time we indulge in gossip we relinquish our personal power. Power comes from power but not all power is positive. Gossip is destructive. So, choose to adhere to the Laws of Mentalism...

Say...I will never decide to do that which will harm another.

Ethics (Laws) of Reciprocity

What we put out there is forever and forever...out there! There is no taking it back and it will travel the ether until it finds whoever is in harmony with it. We must strive to be ethical and discreet in all our endeavors. Keeping your darkest and dearest secrets to yourself is important. It keeps you safe. Show others the same consideration and guard their secrets to keep them safe. Every form of religion worldwide has a rule similar to the Golden Rule. "Do unto others as you would have done unto you." Some examples:

? "The sage has no interest of his own but takes the interests of the people as his own. He is kind to the kind; he is also kind to the unkind:

for Virtue is kind. He is faithful to the faithful; he is also faithful to the unfaithful: for Virtue is faithful." Tao Teh Ching, Chapter 49.

? "Whatever is disagreeable to yourself do not do unto others." Shayast-na-Shayast 13:29

? Socrates: "Do not do to others that which would anger you if others did it to you." (Greece; 5th century). ReligiousTolerance.org

It is not selfish to view your actions as that which should be conducted in a manner that preserves the self and your integrity. It is in fact, wise! For in so doing you will guard against any action that may harm another to prevent harm from coming to you. If you are fully committed to preserving the self and your peace you will act as a peacemaker. There is great power in living a life of peace. Such power transcends the darkness. When you have reached a higher vibration, you must do everything you can to preserve it. Raphael intends to teach you methods of raising your vibration higher in a manner that is easy and yet...it takes great effort to sustain that vibration.

Thus, you may have noticed a repeated theme in this book (I too have noticed as I wait for inspiring words to come) and that it is apparent there are Universal Laws that must be followed if we desire to keep our healing vibrations high. The ebb and flow of the power that comes from a higher vibratory field is not constant. It like all things of the universe is in a state of change. Energy flows like waves in the ocean. In fact, waves in the ocean are affected by the flows of energy that surround us, just like we are. We as light beings must stay abreast of the flows, anticipate them, and correct them if a frequency has come into our space that can disrupt our vibration in a negative way.

The higher our frequency the greater our power, health, capacity to love and accept love. Love is an energy remember. It is not an emotion. Striving to keep our frequency high ensures that we are stable because a higher vibration is stronger...even in the face of adversity. A higher vibration is stable and less easily influenced. The greatest threat to our stability is our thought life...just as the mind controls the body, the mind controls the vibrational field that is us. Likewise, that is how we affect the collective consciousness with our thoughts because are all one with the energy of the universe.

The universal field is the source of our power. Our energy does not come from relationships with others. Nor does it come from the planet as the source of the planet's energy is likewise the universal field. Limited capacity to fully grasp the universes and cosmos, makes the theory of Quantum physics hard to understand.

And now I am learning that the theory is too limiting in its scope. The string theory seems to get more attention. The interaction of all the atoms is the same energy that is us. But what source of power is there beyond the Quantum field? It is limitless, infinite, and eternal. That just boggles the mind. So, I just simply accept that in all its limitlessness that all that power is available whenever needed. If it is limitless then that means, there are no limits to its provision as well. It is easier for a finite mind to accept in a childlike faith that the universe will always provide, will always have our backs, and will always assist us in learning how to take even more energy to use for my personal and highest good. Whenever I experience regret or guilt then I have relinquished a bit of my power. Since there is no judgement within the field, only natural reciprocal action, or vibration, I need not experience guilt. I continue in love directed toward myself and therefore can expect loving energy to flow to and through me. When I live my life in accordance with my highest good, then I am naturally and effortlessly creating a higher form of consciousness within the same field that sustains me. The Ethics of Reciprocity (or laws) are natural as the universe reacts just as it is designed to do. The universe cannot change that, but only to increase in power.

I am going out on a limb here to some extent, but I have been thinking about the universe and universes we know exist. I have been taught for years that energy conducted for healing will follow the laws of the universal energies which flow in a circular motion. Try to think of some energy pattern that does not move in a circle. I considered the crashing of waves on a beach that move in and out but then understood that it was the circular movement of the planet that creates the waves in the first place.

Try to think of an energy pattern within your body that is not circular. Breathing for example. Your life's blood flows in a circular motion from your heart to all cells in your body and then back again. Raphael posed the question to me, "What energy can you think of that moves in a straight line then back again or back and forth? If you can describe one, it would be an energy that caused death because all healing energy moves in a circular motion." To elaborate, if during a healing session, I used an energetic frequency that I visualized as parallel straight lines and then projected that frequency into a client, I would bring a total disruption to the natural life force producing flow of circular motion. On the other hand, I could use such a frequency to destroy, say a cancer, but I would not want to use such a pattern for healing or raising a vibration. So, if all energy flows in a circular motion, then from where does it originate? It is not God per se because as we understand the God concept, he was the creator of it, so he came before it. Is God then the Source in some astounding way? Does it emanate out from Him as the center? Energy that moves in a circular motion finds its origins in a center. Then, did he create it with an intent to see it grow exponentially over billions of years? And now we have this inexplicable source of limitless dimensions? It would naturally have changed for that is nature of energy. It cannot be destroyed but it can be changed.

So, I query, did he merely create a central source of healing power that would sustain the universes forever? If he did, would it not have to be the sun? I began to wonder about it when I was making moon energized water. That is placing glass bottles of water in the light of a full moon for at least three hours (some people worship the moon). While placing the jars, Gabriel asked, "Why us the moon when the light from the moon is merely a reflection of light or power from the sun?" Then, why not energize my water in the daytime when the energy is more powerful? The sun is the center of our universe, and it is our initial source of power and that likely includes healing power.

It was just a thought, but I believe it has credence. So, in knowing that the inspiration of the sun as a source of healing was offered for my consideration; I did some research. Just as the Law of Mentalism works, I began to receive blips from a variety of sources that were directing my research toward pertinent information. Plausible search terms if you are interested are:

Pineal gland and the Sun

Sun as electromagnetic

Sun as most powerful in its power at sunrise.

Hint: Leave water out at night to catch the first morning's rays of power.

Sun Gods and Worshippers

Time was that many worshipped the sun from its lifegiving power. Nothing can survive without light except utter darkness. See the correlation? When the light of the heavens permeates the earth, everything flourishes and yet without balance of darkness/nighttime and rain/water everything would roast into ashes. Imagine the intricacies that are required to create such a magnificent universe! What comes when light shines? Life. Yes, life beginning at the tiniest amoeba to the gigantic mass of a forest large enough to cover an entire continent. If our two most essential elements are light and water, does it not make sense that to combine the two would bring healing at a faster rate?

Couple that with oxygen rich air and the healing would greatly accelerate. Taken a step further, if one added color to the energized water, natural food color, then the colors of the rainbow chakral energy would serve to magnify the waters power even further.

Videos:

Dancing with Water[1] Very interesting perspective on water's informational network.

If we can invoke the moon to provide healing energies that can potentiate our water or our minds, how much more effective/powerful would invoking the sun be when healing? After all, the sun is our primary source of power and should it ever 'burn' out the entire planet would shortly thereafter perish. I had never considered energizing water with the suns illuminating rays until now. I did some research again and found that experiments have been conducted on the matter. It was theorized that water could be altered to enhance the sprouting of seeds, the growth of vegetable plants and alter the immune system of humans. The results are nothing less than impressive particularly when colored filters are applied the bottles of water during exposure to sunlight.

The impetus of the research was to determine if water could be purified for use in areas where clean water is not available. According to reports in the National Institute of Health library of research material-The theory proved correct! Even though the concept is new to me, it is not new to many others. In particular in the United Kingdom where many of the experiments have been conducted. And, to my delight, I discovered that energy healers have been using the water for some time now, and though their numbers are small it is significant that the effects of sun energized are established. When one considers the ramifications, it is staggering to speculate the potential for use of such water in the future. Water that is energized free of charge would save countless lives around the world.

Lengthy research cited because it is indeed worth the time to read it.

National library of medicine We found that water exposed to visible spectral emissions of sunlight had an altered elemental composition, electrical conductance, osmolarity and salt-solubility, as well as differences in biomodulatory effects. The process is dependent upon

---

1. https://www.dancingwithwater.com/

the composition of the vessel, as well as intensity and time of exposure [2]. Placing bottled (plastic/glass) water in sunlight for a minimum of 5 hrs and up to a maximum of 48 hrs has been scientifically shown to detoxify and decontaminate water infected with bacteria and viruses [3–5]. Extended times of exposure to sunlight for approximately six weeks, has been used for solarization of soil [6].

In ancient times, water, after exposure to direct sunlight and filtered through colored glass, was used as a therapeutic modality [8]. The action of sunlight on bottled water, as used in the sterilization study, had been reported as irreversible and documented by the inability of coliforms to re-grow after placing the exposed bottled water in the dark storage [http://almashriq.hiof.no/lebanon/600/610/614/solar-water/unesco/35- 46.html] #8 above ancient times

As true to the idea behind this book, we are inspired by guides and ethereal entities with perceptions of how energy can be better utilized in healing. The act of energizing my water with sun light is a powerful example How is the water different from regular tap or bottled water? Experiments have been conducted that verify the energizing effect of solar irradiation on water. https://www.ncbi.nlm.nih.gov/pmc/articles/PMC3810624/ and National Center for Biotechnology Information NCBI NIH

1.United States researchers found that water exposed to visible spectral emissions of sunlight had an altered elemental composition, electrical conductance, osmolarity and salt-solubility, as well as differences in bio-modulatory effects.

2. Water alone has also shown potential for healing. Healing with water containing various additives as calcium chloride, magnesium sulfate, sodium metasilicate and sulfated castor oil has been patented by Willard AKA Willard Water™

3. In ancient times, water, after exposure to direct sunlight and filtered through colored glass, was used as a therapeutic modality [8].

4. The action of sunlight on bottled water, as used in the sterilization study, had been reported as irreversible and documented by the inability of coliforms to re-grow after placing the exposed bottled water in the dark storage.

5. Abstract from the study states: We investigated the changes in the properties of water when exposed to sunlight for 40 days. We hypothesize and prove that solar irradiation to water entraps electromagnetic radiation as potential energy, which becomes kinetic energy in various systems. It is postulated that photochemically induced energy transfers, associated with individual spectral emission of visible spectrum of solar light, exert diverse influences on biological systems. Bottles of distilled water individually wrapped in spectral-colored cellophane were exposed to sunlight and compared to an unwrapped bottle to determine chemical and physical changes as well as modifications of biological properties.

Each bottle of water was named according to the color of cellophane paper with letter E (stands for exposed) as a prefix with (E-violet, E-indigo, E-blue, E-green, E-yellow, E-orange, and E-red). E-control (without wrap) was exposed to polychromatic sunlight. This study addresses two main issues viz., the chemical and physical changes in E-water and its effect on biological activities. Chemical and physical composition analysis using inductively coupled plasma atomic emission spectrometry; physical conductance by a Wheatstone Bridge type conductivity meter; osmolarity by a vapor pressure osmometer; and salt solubility profile of 10% sodium bicarbonate were determined. Furthermore, testing the effect of E-waters on human lymphocyte proliferation, mosquito larvae hatching, and seed germination determined the functional role of solar radiation through specific spectrum/s of visible light on various biological processes. We found that water exposed to visible spectral emissions of sunlight had an altered elemental composition, electrical conductance, osmolarity and salt-solubility, as well as differences in bio-modulatory effects. A gradual increase in leaching of Boron from E-violet to E-red was noted. E-indigo showed maximal increase in electrical conductance and maximal salt solubility of sodium bicarbonate. E-blue inhibited phyto-hemagglutinin-induced immune cell proliferation and mosquito larvae hatching. E-orange stimulated root elongation in seed germination. We conclude that 40-day exposure of water to specific solar spectrum changes chemical and physical properties and influences on biological activity.

Energizing the water changes the structure of the water molecules back to its original form which is the form most utilized by our body's cells. One of the most dramatic examples I have found to date is contained within a video by Gaia.com entitled The Secret of Water. Not only is the video professionally done, it examines scientific validation of the effects of energy on water, including but not limited to thought energy that was projected toward the water in a container. Gaia.com is a paid subscription. You can sign up for a trial for 30 days for .99 cents to determine the value.

Life is reflected in the life of water. We must learn to be the water and mimic its value to all others, its ability to go with the flow, be forgiving and resilient like water, and then as a drop of water into a pond, at death, simply become one again with the River of Life. Power is not often granted to those who have no outlet or use of it. Thus, finding your ability to be purposeful like water will grant that you will be given power so that you may affect the lives of those around you. Your own water content within your body is a conduit for healing energy to flow through. If water absorbs the energy of that which is around it then the patient's body (of water) will absorb the healing energy you offer because it has no other choice. Water absorbs energy and holds it because it is supposed to so when you heal, be fully hydrated, and make sure your client is too. Note: (Deionized water is faster absorbed) but contains no minerals so it will pull the minerals from your body to return itself to balance.

Given that our bodies are about 65% water, it only makes sense that the more energized water we consume, the healthier we will be. Energized or structured water is water in a natural or original state. Its molecules have form that begin with a hexagonal shape or a six-sided form and as the branches of cells grow out from the center, intricately beautiful shapes like snowflakes form. Evidence indicates that when we consume structured pure water our blood becomes more fluid and less stuck together. Our bodies are compatible with structured or natural water, but it is forced to utilize inferior water to stay alive because that is what we have for our water source now. And energized water can and should be used as an important healing modality.

Water retains the vibration of the planet because it has a memory that can no longer be disputed as relevant to life-giving water sources. I understand that as water flows over the surface of earth it absorbs the frequency it is exposed to. For example, the Schumman Resonances, now recognized as the frequency that is conducted at the planet's surface and resonates with all life here. Our bodies match the frequency of the planet's resonances, and water is structured naturally at the same frequency because it conducts ELF's, low frequency electricity. Therefore, the theoretical evidence is growing that as we consume structured water our own electromagnetic field grows stronger and weak spots begin to disappear. Weak spots are often found near or around vital organs such as the liver, pancreas, and brain. The same resonances are also known to be foundational to human consciousness. The importance of structured water becomes even more evident when we consider the brain is 73% water and that the brain controls the entire body. Consciousness is not in the brain; it is the essence of the individual housed in the body the memory is not located in the brain it is consciousness. As a layperson, I understand electromagnetic radiation to be a wave of photons with a certain frequency, and different frequencies have different characteristics to us.

For example, we can detect with our eyes, certain frequencies, but others we cannot, even if they can cause otherwise visible effects (such as heating something up). A magnetic field, however, I imagine as something like a "force field" that attracts or repels things, which we can fluctuate to do work such as spin a rotor. Water maintains the body as long as it is in physical form.

"The Schumann resonances (SR) are a set of spectrum peaks in the extremely low frequency (ELF) portion of the Earth's electromagnetic field spectrum. Schumann resonances are global electromagnetic resonances, generated and excited by lightning discharges in the cavity formed by the Earth's surface and the ionosphere. Which is 56-59 miles out to edge of ionosphere."

Latest advances if water purification systems.

Innovative water filtration system ideas are surfacing with increasing speed as more organizations rally to find ways in which we can filter out harmful metals and pollutants from our water supply. Water is indeed becoming scarcer as our needs and use of water expands at alarming rates.

Solar irradiation to kill bacteria that are life threatening.

The World Health Organization estimates 3,575,000 people die every year from water related illnesses. Of those who die annually, 2.2 million are children. http://www.who.int/quantifying_ehimpacts/ publications/saferwater/en/index.html
http://water.org/learn-about-the-water-crisis/facts/
? World Health Organization report: Safer water, better health[2]

---

2. https://www.bing.com/aclk?ld=e819HHQom1MaNw9o-Meo3MFjVUCUyFz-

Jy_qNVlRSWyWQDu1FmgUF7fP9NCbhldckbq_x7LC3FOZ5xsF4Fq4QvxZIvIfGVcLTBs2

P_TV-LLrQRFClMijnjFS3GQ_TuCIgLeWh64CB6ukQeU1TB-

qGQZPg7SpftpfoW6LbUqmmaTLw46ebR-

2V5ZdYI1BHDjnqipf5_cQ&u=aHR0cHMlM2ElMmYlMmZsaWZldG9kYXkub3JnJTJmY2

? Water.org:[3] Learn about the water crisis

Given those facts are disturbing to say the least, as a healer or concerned individual, take seriously the positive effects of drinking structured water and how healing can be enhanced by the use and ingestion of it during a healing session. Dr. Robert O. Becker in his book The Body Electric establishes that the human body has an electrical frequency and that much about a person's health can be determined by its frequency.

In 1992, Bruce Tainio of Tainio Technology, an independent division of Eastern State University in Cheny, Washington, built the first frequency monitor in the world. Tainio has determined that the average frequency of the human body during the daytime is 62-68 Hz. (A healthy body frequency is 62-72 Hz.) When the frequency drops, the immune system is compromised. If the frequency drops to 58 Hz, cold and flu symptoms appear, at 55 Hz, diseases like Candida take hold, at 52 Hz, Epstein Bar and at 42 Hz,

Cancer. According to Dr. Royal R. Rife, every disease has a frequency. He found that certain frequencies can prevent development of disease and that others would destroy disease. Substances with higher frequency will destroy diseases of a lower frequency. The study of frequencies raises important questions concerning the frequencies of substances we eat, breathe, and absorb. Many pollutants lower healthy frequency.

Processed/canned foods have a frequency of zero. Fresh produce has up to 15 Hz, dry herbs from 12 to 22 Hz, and fresh herbs from 20 to 27 Hz. Essential oils start at 52 Hz and go as high as 320 Hz, which is the frequency of Rose oil. Clinical research shows that essential oils have

---

xlYW53YXRlciUzZnV0bV9zb3VyY2UlM2RiaW5nJTI2dXRtX211ZGl1bSUzGNwYyUyNn
V0bV9jYW1wYWlnbiUzZExPSV9XRkxxfQWNxdWlzaXRpb25fMDFfMjAyMl9CaW5nU2
VhcmNoXzNNQJTI2bXNjbGtpZCUzZGJiNTk5YTczMjlhMDFiOTEzYmEzZjg3ZTY4ZTli
NzI0&rlid=bb599a7329a01b913ba3f87e68e9b724&ntb=1

3. https://water.org/

the highest frequency of any natural substance known to man, creating an environment in which disease, bacteria, virus, fungus, etc., cannot live.

In fact, clinical research has proven that 100% pure essential oils are immune stimulating. Moreover, other research shows that many of the "super bugs" that has modern medicine so concerned, cannot survive in the presence of essential oils...nor has there been any pathogen known to resist them by mutating.

Dr. Masaru Emoto's work is well known and here are two fine examples of his discoveries. Dr. Masaru Emoto and Water Consciousness (thewellnessenterprise.com)[4]

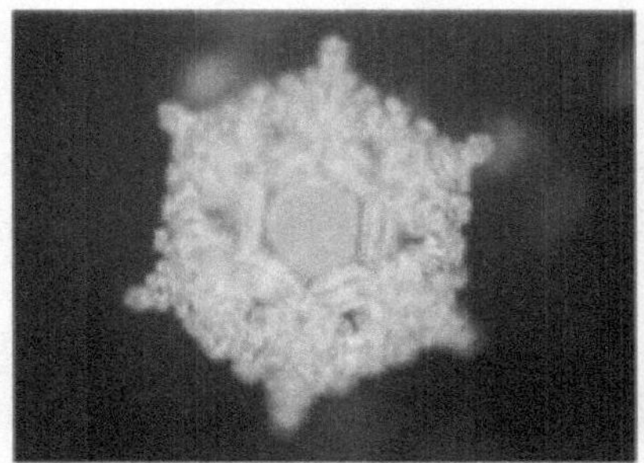

Love and Gratitude

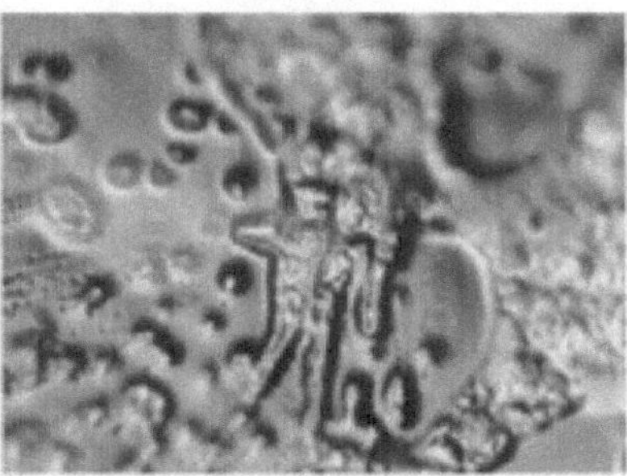

You Disgust Me

A water crystal that is intended or programmed with Love and Gratitude versus the one on the right which is programmed with disgust.

Now we are at a point of tying all the information together to see what kind of picture one wants to paint with the tools and medium provided. Once a person has seen the path that they are to take, such as inspired ideas while reading, just like I stated in the beginning of the book, then the practice and the tools will be presented. The methods employed by shamans are those that defy the logic of the average thinker.

---

4. https://thewellnessenterprise.com/emoto/

The shaman lives in a state of inspired and directed thought and the messages conveyed are always relevant no matter irrelevant they may seem. One piece of copper for example interwoven with crystals and symbols becomes a healing device. A feather from a powerful bird can be used to free a sickened mind by increasing the limitlessness of that minds reach. When choices for future endeavors are narrowed down to the most significant of items that are more powerful than others to choose from then of course the most powerful tools will become the companion tools of Today's Shaman.

That which does not seem to possess the positive energy or heightened energy of a shaman's tool is then laid aside and the new more energetic item is tucked within the belt of the healer until it is revealed to the universe as the path for healing energy to be conducted into. Every tool a shaman uses must be created personally by the shaman and the energy of the shaman must be implanted firmly into it and set strong with lasting intentions of purpose and power. Shamans are gifts to the universe because they can interact with properties that are ordinarily isolated from mankind The love a healer puts into the work they do creates a lasting bond with the field that enlivens everything and restores all that is weakened. Few are they who can arrange for a private parlay with the hosts of heaven and expect to gain an audience of the most magnanimous kind.

Because the healer is always a bit ahead of their time, their time is always right for change and integral adjustments in energetic patterns that are forming and formulating to create a new paradigm shift in consciousness as only the shaman can. Why is this so? Shamans are born to this. It is that simple. Wrestling with the details of this matter is nonsensical because this is one of the times when one just accepts what is. If one is called to be a healer, it will be apparent they have the gift of healing. If one is designated to be a shaman, then the course of their life will reflect a different set of gifts that are not usual. It could be that communication on a level that is not customary for spiritualists will become self-evident and the person will seem to just know they are different. The difference they feel is not to be confused with not fitting in, but the knowledge that a profound difference exists and is meant to be.

This awareness is not meant to create a feeling of superiority, in fact, it should instill the opposite wherein the called feels a deep sense of humility and responsibility to his or her calling. Oftentimes, the knowledge of a calling to shamanism is met with a bit fear and trepidation as the awareness of the role that is intended is not to be taken lightly. The passage, "For unto whomsoever much is given, of him shall be much required," Luke 12:48 in the King James Version conveys the gravity of the gifts and the tasks.

It is imperative to remind you that the needs created by the tasks suggested shall be met with provision and support of spiritual gifts and power.

Nor are those who are selected expected to be an island in a sea of troubles and storms that can press upon them to the point of fear. No, fear is not a point at all but a serious approach to the call and the action is of the utmost importance. Here at this juncture, one must ask the self...am I ready for this?

Chapter Seven: Tools of today's shaman

Amongst the planes of thought are many varying degrees of maturity and maturation is imperative to wellness and wholeness. The very idea that one can heal their body by controlling their mind is not new, but it is newer than the idea of using strictly a chemical prescription process of correcting a non-chemical entity. You see, man or the humankind is not comprised of a chemical makeup. It is instead, purely energy and therefore, energy is what is required to correct any sort of malformation or malfunction in the energetic pattern that comprises the person.

The body is merely a vehicle the mind uses to create and maintain mobility throughout the life process. If the body is not functioning optimally then the symptom of illness is nothing more than a lower or too low vibration within the field in the mind and the body. This is straightforward and simplistic by definition; however, it is in simplicity that the mind constructs the process of wholeness and powerful vibration that is capable of creating and maintaining a state of wellness. What one thinks one becomes and therefore if one thinks about illness and fears it because they feel inept to heal it then one becomes and remains ill because the body has become programmed to be ill. Likewise, if the mind seeks and trusts in a state of wellness and power then the body remains strong. The vibration of the body is equal to the power of thought created in the mind.

Resonance of the mind of body are akin to the field inside and outside the mind. However, the mind is the field, and the field is the mind. The two coexist and are as one just as all people are all one. It is easy to grasp if one sees the wholeness of the universe as one tiny dot in the atmosphere of energetic patterns and vibrations and not as too vast universal in scope to fathom without personalizing the universe into the separate factions of individuals. Wholeness and oneness are the same when one considers the power of the mind to heal or to make the sick the body.

Bad vibrations are simply low vibrations of powerlessness such as fear, anger, disillusionment, disgust, discouragement, and the similar terms are permeated by negative or illness producing vibrations and an energy that is too weak to harbor high density and unified vibrations that bring about a state of great health, logic, steadfastness, and stability. You will recall the conversation of earlier of the desire people have to be near others who are stable and dependable. Conversely, they avoid the chaos and drama of one who is determined to pull away their energy because they are too ignorant to have created their own wellness and power. Power is essential, and power comes from the heightened awareness of having experienced the state of wellness even in light of darkness surrounding the one who is powerful or full of power.

The second may be a better way of explaining how wellness pervades the body when the energy is high and dissipates when the energy or thought power has decreased or maybe ever failed to manifest in the one's experiences. When one learns that they can create wellness by reprogramming their mind they have to experience some sort of manifestation of the possibility or witness the same in another that enables them to cast off the feeling of helplessness for an empowering alternative of taking responsibility for their own health.

Information leads to contemplation, then contemplation leads to practice and practice leads to experience and experience to retention of the knowledge of the power one possesses. It starts small normally and it progresses through a series of trials and once one is convinced, they retain the power they affect through belief and knowledge of a new reality then the truth of power to control one's life is manifest in a new sense of freedom from fear and weakness. Even the most vulnerable person can overcome fear and weakness if they determine to accept the possibility of change.

Oddly, it is all in the manner in which one thinks and yet, if old patterns of thought hold one in chains of the past then the person will first have to alter the memories to positivity and relegate the chaos of the past to the past where it can no longer affect the present with its limiting and chaotic vibrations. Thoughts are patterned after habitual manners of thought. Responses are predictable and unchanging in a person who still thinks the same way they did when their personality was forming. Hence, maturity versus immaturity of the thought process is evident in one who is emotional and over-reactive or unstable. Emotions are regulatory and act as a barometer of sorts that alerts people to harm, causes them to reach out in love, makes life interesting if disruption is inviting and exciting if drama is present.

Emotions are evidently the measure of humanness that many desire as that which makes them more interesting than another or more important than most. Emotions are for the needy and fearful. Logic and accountability are symptoms of a mature and focused mind. Awareness results from having found the sense of power that connects man to the field of the mind and the field of energy that comprises the universe and its all-inclusive power source of imagination and creation. In light of the limitlessness of the power available, one can surmise nearly anything is possible if it can be understood as purposeful and honest in its intent.

The tools of the shaman are so numerous with respect to how often the shaman connects and defines the intent of the universe and then coincides his or her intent with the pattern of energy and thought being revealed. If one is truly connected to the field of thought that pervades the universe, then that one will be acting on accordance with the design of the universes creative power and that power is about wholeness or wellness. It is not that the field would ever limit the power or vibration available to any who choose to heal because it would go totally contrary to the very nature of the field to do so. The conflict comes from the lack of resolution of the mind of the one attempting to create (anything).

The loss of effectual results is the basis for doubt and yet doubt has no place in the field, therefore if it exists only in the mind of the creator, it is from the mind it must be removed and then be replaced with intention that is set firmly in the knowledge that the creation is possible. Healing as presented by a shaman is not impossible to attain even if the client has no faith in the healing power of intention and direction of energy to an end means or body part or tissue of any material sort. Matter is so easily adjusted to a position of wellness just as it is easily adjusted to a malformation of illness. Matter's ideal state is whole and healed. Its origin was well and so can be its present state when the energy to create wholeness is reunited with the energy that was present at the time of inception (birth). (Death is not the same as we are talking about, death is fulfillment of the mission or purpose here) Reunification of the original and present energetic states is obvious as it means returning the body to its perfect state of being even though aging will be apparent. As long as we live in the types of bodies we presently possess, we will be subject to aging and the death process.

If we transcend and become enlightened, we may still want to use the body as a vehicle to learn and transcend to an even higher state that will eventually satisfy our soul. We can move through the dimensions of reality and perception in other ways, but the human experience has been historically the most successful to date on Earth. To delve into the varieties of ways one may use to transcend would take another book... The movement we are experiencing now regarding our ability to heal references the ability we have to learn to recreate our lives and in so doing we recreate our body too. It is the way we think that made us sick. So, learning to think differently and with healing as an addendum or given, will bring about a state of being that one has not experienced before.

It is becoming the master of your thoughts, actions and reactions and retaining the knowledge and wisdom that you only need to accept the flow of energy you are offered to receive it. When you have surrendered your foolish notions about energetic promise and delivery based upon your childhood memories and actions, you will discover that the new memories you create of magical change and renewal are the new you. Your choices will be different. Your life will be different. You will become nothing of importance because you will have accepted fully the concept of being part of a whole...one amongst the Oneness of All Things. Great wisdom lies in knowing that there is nothing in life that brings fear if you do not embrace it. If you have been conditioned to embrace fear, then when you change your conditioning to the new fearless way of life you intend to live then the Universe will bow to meet you.

Without a particle of belief in your mind at this point it is senseless to endeavor to create a whole new life in a matter of months or years. It takes a lifetime to recreate a lifetime. If only people could find a way to allow others to believe in that which would enslave less and free more. All the attitudes of life on Earth are centered upon getting ahead of another or simply getting ahead in a manner that has become so prevalent that it consumes people's lives and all possibility. Life becomes one of doing and far too little of being.

Being is like the universe in its completed form. It is of such beauty and wonder and all of it is exposed. Life is so similar for all, that exposure is necessary to create an ideal form of living that promotes expansion and inclusion for everyone. A specific platform or foundation of life exists, and it is one all can practice. It does not mean that everyone is the same or robotic. It means that a successful model has been constructed over the many millennia of man's existences. That may sound confusing or even undesirable. For one to understand the limitlessness of the

Universe is beyond comprehension because everyone is always learning, gaining information, and transfiguring after absorbing new experiences into their being.

In other words, you never stop changing and expanding your mind. You will never arrive; you will keep going onward to another and then another destination. If this were not so, who would want to be eternal? Who could want to be eternally the same? Peace may be primary on the minds of most who are seeking refining and reintegration into a more advanced way of thought and definitive way of acting. Peace is not yet within the grasp of living beings. Peace evades all because the concept of the conqueror conquering is still pervasive in the universes. If this changes then what? If all life was concerned for the well-being of all other life, what would living be like?

These poignant questions are worth considering and pondering because if you can wrap your mind around the potential for such, you will have dispelled most of the lies you have been conditioned to believe and think of as reality. In order to change the mind to promote possibility, the lies must be purged. The memories must be exposed as perceptions of moments but likely not reality at all. One cannot see the world through a child's eyes and expect to be wise or mature. Our lifetime of memories is formulated and even tainted by our perception of the moment when we have not renewed our perceptions at a young age.

The perceptions we form will be the perceptions we utilize to interpret our world. When, in fact, the world may be nothing at all like we have conditioned ourselves to perceive it. Memories are like little moments of deception if one had a bad experience that even remotely related to the situation at any time prior to the incident. It is like the mind reacts with, "Oh, here we go again. I was hurt the first time this type of event took place, and it will be the same form now on in any similar events. So, I have to be prepared to defend or protect myself. Therefore, my defenses will be up, and my adrenaline will start pumping because

I am stressed by my perception, *even if the situation is in actuality harmless.*" The similarity is the trigger of another memory related to the perception.

Changing perceptions is then vital to reconditioning the mind. Raphael referenced the need to be less emotional. He even alluded to being emotionless in order to be a higher thought being. It is so easy to reference Spock on Star Trek because he was purely logical and interpreted all situations from the perception of logic and not based upon his reaction to the event or situation. He remained calm and offered advice to Captain Kirk that was sound. It is hard to imagine life without emotion and it is also a little impossible to think we may want to be emotionless. After all, emotion is fun if it is healthy fun such as laughter, joy, elation, awe, or feelings that are similar, such positive emotions are positive frequencies. Whereas anger is not a positive emotion. It causes a stress response which causes adrenaline to flow and enhances a conditioned response because we are human, and our minds are designed to function and preserve us like animals.

Fight or flight...we are all familiar with the theory. And yet, to acknowledge that we are more like the animal kingdom than we readily admit to is not so familiar. We place ourselves far above the animal world even though our behaviors are in many ways similar. It is apparent that animals have emotions just like we do. What remains to be determined is how closely our brains resemble that of an animal. Animals have memories. Would we then surmise that they have a soul as well? The latest theories are that memories are not located in our brains. Biologist, author, and investigator Dr. Rupert Sheldrake notes that the search for the mind has gone in two opposite directions.

While a majority of scientists have been searching inside the skull, he looks outside. At least when memory is stimulated it does not show up on brain wave patterns when tracked. So, the theory of healing memories is in fact, healing the soul and allowing spiritual growth to replace negative memories that bind people to a closed perception of the world and universe. If the soul is the home of the memory, that should make it much easier to heal than the brain would be. It could be as simple as adjusting the energy pattern of the soul/memory and clearing it to allow for expansion of the thought process.

When the brain retains an energetic pattern, it becomes the same, a pattern. A pattern of thought, reaction, contemplation, and rumination. It goes around and round again ever repeating the same pattern/reaction whether the response be positive or negative depends on the nature of the memory. The key to remember is that it is an established pattern of thought/energy. The pattern must be altered to halt the pattern. For example, every time a woman hears a baby cry her mind responds with attention until it is determined that the cry is not that of her child. Then the attention is dismissed as unnecessary. Over time, when a woman is no longer having and raising children, the absence of the crying baby will lessen or un-condition the attention/action response from the woman.

Within the range of the new healing energy, we are being offered the memory can be unconditioned using deliberate action such as deleting then storing the memory in a cloud just like one does with files in a computer. I must explain this process thoroughly.

A story:

I was employed in a retail setting that employed people who were not awakened. The negativity in that location was complex and difficult to cope with because I was not used to working in that type of environment. As a result of the influences of so many low vibrations and the strange habit many had of ridiculing one another keeping a positive outlook and thought pattern was difficult. Over time, I years. I tried to control it but the negativity was so pervasive it was hard to manage. I turned to my guides for advice. Archangel Michael responded with this plan.

"You know that any files on your computer you do not want to see can be stored away in a cloud. The same can be done with the files in your mind. Create a cloud above your head that will go with your everywhere you go. Whenever you are bothered by a pesky thought, simply use your swirling hand to create a vortex above your head and gather that memory into the vortex. Then say, I am done with this thought, Leave and never bother me again. I send you into my cloud. Then with a flick of the wrist flip the memory into the cloud. Though is merely energy remember and it can be controlled in such a manner. The cloud will eventually become darkened abut over time the memories will be deleted from your field, never to return."

Try it! It really works.

Interestingly, the files of deleted memories are after a bit of time, as the response to them is, let's say forgotten, yes, that makes sense, the memory will be permanently deleted from the cloud. Furthermore, the cloud acts as a shield and filters similar thoughts projected by others into the collective consciousness. Unfortunately, most people are not aware they can control their thought and are thus controlled by them.

I teach a course about the Transformation Orbit of the Mind. It explains how anyone can easily project a minimizing thought into a cloud above their head. It also focused on creating our life in a living vision board

Therefore, by the action of deleting a memory from the mind to the clouds ensures the energy created by such mutual thought patterns is annulled and the person is now free to move on into a new life's pattern of thought. That new pattern can be anything from childlike to philosopher, depending on the desires and pursuits of the individual. The possibilities are limitless. The probability of one learning this on their own is low, therefore healers are needed to assist others along their way to higher thought.

~What you seek is seeking you. -Rumi

It may surprise most healers to know that what gifts you require to perform amazing healings are yours for the asking. We are no longer in the position of pleading or supplicating the heavens for power and wisdom. In fact, most angels and guides want us to be fully aware of the fact that they are seeking those who will accept such gifts. We are moving into a period of enlightenment and in such a period we will have access to energy that can have a huge impact on the world and its inhabitants. It is the positive impact that is being pursued that has perpetuated the availability of power unlike we have seen before. That power is what will supply the tools we Shamans seek and the healing that our clients require.

For each healing or energy session performed the world will be altered a bit and each bit will become greater in affect. It is not like we hope we have an influence on the condition or state of things and situations, but that we know we do. It is the knowing that is propelling the collective consciousness and it is the collective consciousness that is propelling us forward with its need for change. So. as we become a tool or instrument of change in service to the All, the All becomes a tool or instrument for our use. We create mutually beneficial energetic patterns that will grow exponentially as we have been told. It is now that we are in the new energetic pattern and higher vibration that we can expect a more rapid response and result. Thus, as Archangel Raphael stated, we will have the energy to rock the world and change it forever. Whether or not you feel as one who is being sought after to help in this endeavor is for you to decide. We are on the cusp of a new day.

The cusp meaning that we are integrating past knowledge into present methods and then expanding the whole of healing into the future. Just as being born on the cusp between two astrological signs equates to one having both characteristics, our integrated energetic healing will offer us new tools such as energetic devices that deliver the proper frequency for healing and pattern shifting in clients and our environment. And we will collectively integrate what they teach us into all that has served us well. We will begin a new fight. Shamans are warriors at heart and the Universe is seeking an army of enlightened warriors who can sense and shift energetic patterns to a more positive vibration by raising it up or quickening it to match the vibration of an empowered world.

"If you want to find the secrets of the universe, think in terms of energy, frequency and vibration."– Nikola Tesla He was so right they murdered him for knowing!

Tools:

The Healing Benefits of Crystals by Amy Crawford

"In recent years, and as part of my own wellness journey, I have been introduced to (and hence forth embraced), the healing power of crystals. I had been 'aware' of crystals in my past life - that being my million-miles-an-hour corporate life (let's say my less spiritually aware life) - yet there was no time or place for them. How much has changed. I was first properly introduced to crystals during my Reiki Practitioner training and these beautiful stones (including the quartz crystals you see above) are now a part of my every day working life. The beauty and power of crystals and other stones have been long recognised, since the dawning of civilization - prized for not only their beauty but for their healing and spiritual power. Healers, shamans and priests have long used crystals for their unique and special properties.

It is widely believed crystals vibrate at the same pitch as humans - such that the resonance between the stone and the human either combats the vibration of the illness or amplifies that of health. More and more humanity is re-discovering this ancient and often forgotten healing and recognising it's part to play in the healing process. In my treatment process, as a CTC or Reiki Practitioners, I use the quartz crystals above to help amplify and balance the energy in the room and to assist in channeling universal life energy. There are thousands of different crystals on the planet but few are used in crystal healing. The easiest way to understand the powers of different crystals is learn the properties of color." (Used with permission: Amy Crawford www.theholisticingredient.com[1]

Links and possibilities to explore:

HAELO: PEMF Frequency Therapy.[2]
This game changing technology delivers the power of symphonic frequencies to optimize your recovery, physical performance, and cellular health.
US Pro 2000 2nd Edition Portable Ultrasound Therapy Device[3]

The **US Pro 2000 2nd Edition** is a clinical grade therapeutic ultrasound device that helps with effective pain relief. The pulsed sound waves travel deep into the tissue and induce vasodilation, which helps increase blood flow to the treated area and is found to help relieve pain and reduce muscle spasms. It comes uniquely equipped with a soundhead pre-warming feature on an ergonomically designed sound head for increased patient comfort. Before starting therapy the soundhead preheats so that it's more comfortable and warm. Once therapy is engaged, the pre-warming feature turns off to allow for the most effective treatment.
Chi Machines.[4]
Benefits of the Chi Machine's therapeutic massage include temporarily relief of minor muscle aches, pains, and tension caused by fatigue or overexertion. It

---

1. http://www.theholisticingredient.com

2. https://www.haelo.com/?rfr=bingads-
   search&msclkid=20e843237d5b1136ad85212c988724d8&utm_source=bing&utm_medium=
   cpc&utm_campaign=HLO%20-
   %20Search%20Sales&utm_term=%2Benergy%20%2Bhealing&utm_content=Search%20New
   %20Users#shopify-section-1631855731ebedef16

3. https://www.tenspros.com/us-pro-2000-portable-ultrasound-
   du3035.html?msclkid=cbc784e0c5a41cc672e3e6ef20785f55

4. https://www.energywellnessproducts.com/
   chimachine.htm?msclkid=44eac0fac6181912d22da2f52c799a9f

temporarily increases circulation. It also locally relaxes muscles promoting a greater sense of well-being! According to an Australian study, it promotes lymphatic drainage and movement. Recent studies have even shown that massage may benefit Anxiety, Stress, Insomnia, Fibromyalgia, Lymphedema, and Headaches.

<u>Considering a Rife Machine? - Resonant Light Technology</u>[5]

<u>Chi Machine - YouTube</u>[6] Become a Chi Machine Distributor <u>(chimachineshop.com)</u>[7]

<u>5 In 1 Professional Ultrasonic Slimming Lipo Laser Cavitation Machine – Generu</u>[8]

Research Topics to pursue if you feel lead to:

1. Energetic Devices
2. Purple plates[9]
3. VoiceBio Analysis Practitioners[10]
4. SCENAR with Rife Etheric Energy Medicine and Frequency Modulation[11]

---

5. https://www.resonantlight.com/
   rife-machine/?matchtype=e&device=c&msclkid=f51ad370d53c150a626fb17a04d92ae5

6. https://www.youtube.com/watch?v=7hhCqdTFqNw&t=6s

7. https://chimachineshop.com/chimachine-distributor.php

8. https://www.generu.co/products/ultimate-5-in-1-ultrasonic-slimming-lipo-laser-cavitation-
   machine?variant=40893043343553&utm_medium=cpc&utm_source=bing&utm_campaign=
   Bing%20Shopping&msclkid=1e647397ccab118696a6119d1f434de1&utm_term=458681892
   0186411&utm_content=5%20in%201%20Cavitation%20Machine

9. https://www.purpleplates.com/

10. https://www.lanajthomas.com/voicebio.html

11. https://www.energy-medicine.org/scenar.html

Navigating the New World

Advice from the Archangels: Strange as it may seem, it will not be easy to be the catalyst the world requires, and it will not be as satisfying as one proposes because the work will be hard. Arduous is the path of a Shaman in the New World. The tasks will be so many that it will be hard to live a normal life of any sort. The energy, though pervasive in the New World is a stronger vibration than most have ever experienced, and it will be felt. It may not bring peace, at first, so, one must always be prepared to adjust the frequency when it dips and restore it to stability before people become ill. We are offering you special protection from harm or detriment if you will agree to bring the power of this energy to the whole of the world. It can be done, and it can have the most amazing effect on everything, everyone and all that exists in this galaxy. We do not propose that you have the power to do these things on your own! Oh, heavens no, we state you will have to keep in constant contact with us, so we can help direct you whenever you need us. In this manner, we can keep you safe and usher you into an even higher vibration than those around you, so you have the connection you will need to move forth through the darkest hour this planet has ever seen. Many will fall victim to instability of the flow of energy that will be created and even though the trials of those who reject the new world will be many, in the end, it will be so obvious that it is, was time for the New World to come into being. Now we will elaborate. If we have not lost your attention at this point, we suspect that you are still interested in taking part in the role of Today's Shaman.

It seems that though the role of shaman has been somewhat respected for many thousands of years. It is now time for the spiritual healer to find their place among the greatest healers of all time. We make really broad claims of how healers can make a difference in the world and in the galaxy and yet we know that without shamans, the changes will never arrive. Why? The shaman is the connection between heaven and earth. Does that seem strange to you to hear that? If so, we are not sure why because it requires one with all spiritual gifts, especially clairaudience to hear the directions that need to be followed and also shamans have been in training for many years, so they would be ready for this time.

Listen to me, listen to the cries of the people and weeping of the lost and forgotten. We see them, we hear them we know them like we know our own friends. We have an ear for their pleas and when the energy shifts have taken place, with your help, we will at last be able to deliver them. Who are they that weep and cry out to us? The masses yes, but still in silence are they that sense we have a place for them. They are the people filled with shadows of times past and memories that make them ache with fear. They are everybody and the anybody's who have always filled this dimension with promise. They are the children of the universe who have been settled into a dream state of inactivity and waiting for a day they know was promised long ago. They are you before you found your way. Now that you have, you have the supreme opportunity to help others find theirs. In a little while, a path will be so well lit that for people to miss it will have to have been by deliberate choice. Those who do not wish to find light will be granted darkness. However, for those who seek light, a beacon will be erected in a way none can miss.

Miracle upon miracle will be performed and light will fill the eyes of those who had lost hope. We just need a few more healers to join our ranks so we can train them to be the best they can be. We present to you at this time the Moses Message. It is time to set the people free. The only thing that can loosen the minds of the ensnared is higher vibrational thought patterns. Hence, we have to be able to control how minds perceive the faithless. The faithless being your current leadership and governing bodies.

They currently control all minds of the lost and ignorant. Their power to persuade the masses to follow them has been broken. Truth comes in light. Honesty is persuasive, and it will set people free from hopelessness and powerlessness. It will imbue the masses with great wealth of new information about how the universe is and will be reaching out to embrace them in the days ahead. Lies and half-truths will no longer have the ability to deceive the intuitive who will be given eyes to see and minds to perceive what lies have done to them all their lives. Freedom of thought results in freedom of spirit and a free spirit can soar above the deception in a manner that their wings in flight will blow away the dust from all eyes and ears. This is true of all who will listen and reach back when a hand reaches for them.

Quoting British physicist Colin McClare, Dr. Bruce Lipton (1) said, "Information can be carried by chemistry, and information can be carried by vibration. The question is whether one is better than the other." Lipton explains that chemical reactions transfer only about two percent of information — 98 percent dissipates as heat loss.

Information transmitted by frequency and vibration (energy) passes nearly 100 percent of the information. Lipton added that chemical signals travel through fluid at a speed of about one foot per second; vibration, resonance, and frequency (sound) travel at 186,000 miles per second. The visionary Rudolf Steiner said that "Pure tones will be used for healing before the end of the [20th] century." Indeed, that has happened, but there is much work to be done in identifying how specific sound and energy frequencies affect the body in specific ways. But with the number of studies underway today, it should not be long before sound therapy technology is embraced by mainstream medicine as a powerful complementary therapy.

? Copper and Gold

? Water ? Empathic Healing

? Tesla and the Rife Machines

? Telepathic and Telekinetic Healing

? Vision and Perception

? Mind Control

? Music and Biofield Tuning

Voice elements respond to sound (tongues and storms) you can only chant in the present One elegant piece of sound healing technology was the inspiration of alternative health practitioner Lilly Whitehawk. Combining her observations of the beneficial effects of specific sound frequencies with her knowledge of quantum physics and physiology, Whitehawk envisioned a healing tool combining ancient knowledge and modern technology. Confirming Maman's findings, Whitehawk observed that the human voice is the most effective for sound healing, followed by singing bowls and tuning forks. (Gaia.com)

Studies show that that this practice, called "sound bathing," directly reduces anxiety and depression; both are related to increases in disease. According to one study.

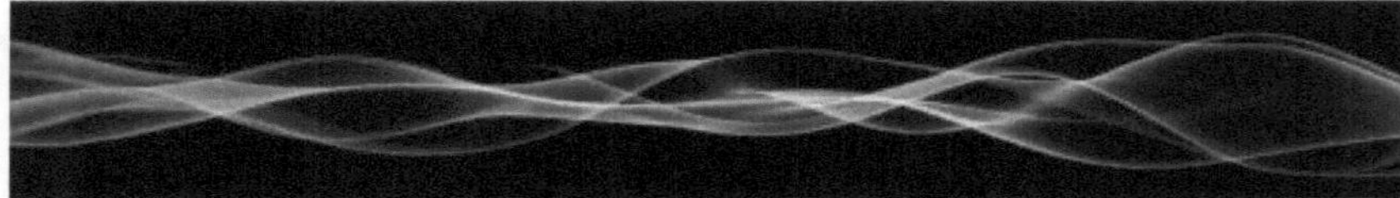

In Closing

The days we serve others are the days we most assuredly serve the self the most. The evolving soul is not made divine by what it does but by what it strives to do. This is true of all who will listen and reach back when a hand reaches for them.

If you wish to contact me:

NuHealing Institute

www.lanajthomas.com[12]

lanajthomas57@gmail.com

Be blessed always and always be a blessing

---

12. http://www.lanajthomas.com

Bibliography

Lipton, B. (2005) Biology of Belief: Unleashing the power of consciousness, matter, and miracles. Mountain of Love Productions. Santa Rosa, CA.

Gaia Staff (2018) Healing with sound, frequency and vibration Biofield Tuning

Healing with Sound, Frequency, and Vibration (biofieldtuning.com)[13]

---

13. https://www.biofieldtuning.com/post/2018/11/21/healing-with-sound-frequency-and-vibration

Don't miss out!

Visit the website below and you can sign up to receive emails whenever Lana J Thomas publishes a new book. There's no charge and no obligation.

https://books2read.com/r/B-A-CQRS-JERWB

BOOKS 2 READ

Connecting independent readers to independent writers.

About the Author

More than 40 years of telepathic commuication with etheric beings and angels has culminated in information sharing by Lana. The goals she strives for are reaching others who wish to be exceptioinal and gifted healers. The wisdom shared with her for her illuminated readers is obvious in her writing, podcasts and videos.

Read more at www.lanajthomas.com.